KAMIKAZE PEACOCKS
& OINK

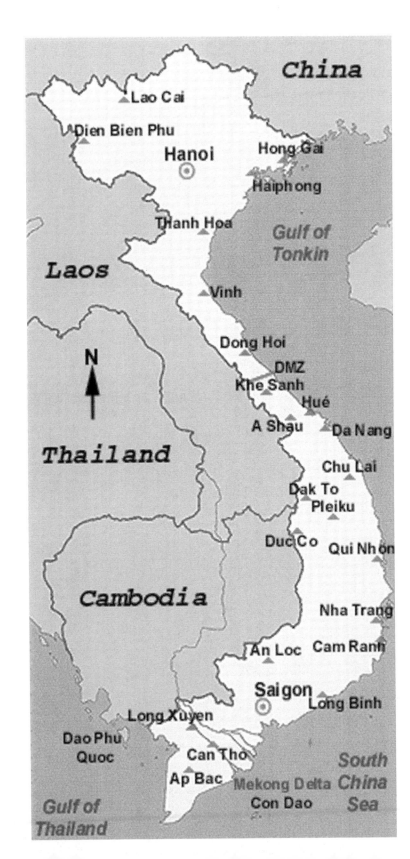

To: Ron & Monica

Have fun & enjoy life !!

KAMIKAZE PEACOCKS & OINK

Coming of Age in an Unfunny War

Peter J. Fournier

ISBN 10: 1492261408
ISBN 13: 978-1492261407

LCCN: 2003098279

This book is intended as an educational and informational resource. The publisher and author expressly disclaim any responsibility or liability in connection with the use of this book.

Publishing Consultant: Sylvia Hemmerly
Interior Design and Typesetting: Publishing Professionals,
    Port Richey, FL
Cover Design: George Foster, Foster Covers

Printed in the United States of America

The paper used in this publication meets the minimum requirements of the American National Standard for Information Sciences—Permanence of Paper for Printed Library Materials, ANSI Z39.48-1984.

Dedication

This book is dedicated to all of my teachers at Millburn High School, Millburn, NJ who insisted that I and my fellow students learn to write logical, coherent English sentences. Were it not for their untiring vigilance, the adjectives, nouns, pronouns, and conjunctions in *Kamikaze Peacocks & Oink* might have merged into an incomprehensible "phở[1] soup."

I especially want to dedicate this work to my Latin teacher, Eugene Kopacz, and to my French teacher, Mlle. Bonjour. They instilled in me an insatiable love of foreign languages and an undying appreciation for other cultures.

I would be remiss if I did not also include my Vietnamese teachers, Dr. Vu Thanh Long and Dr. Vu Tam Ich, in this dedication. Their enthusiasm and love of teaching enabled me to experience worlds previously known only in the far reaches of my imagination.

---

1.   Vietnamese noodles served with beef, chicken, etc.

Table of Contents

Preface & Disclaimer

This book was written in response to many requests from friends and relatives. Whenever we would have parties or family get-togethers, I would be asked to tell some of my Vietnam stories. However, after many years of telling and retelling, I was encouraged to put my narratives in writing.

The stories in this book are written completely from memory. Most of them took place during the height of the Vietnam War, namely 1964 through 1968. I admit that many of the dates and places may be dead wrong. In most cases, that is totally immaterial. The facts of the incidents are true; I have embellished several of them slightly for effect. All of the names have been changed to protect those that I worked with.

I returned from Vietnam a very sad and broken man. The war tore my heart out. During my duties as a translator/interrogator/interpreter, I encountered many grim and gruesome scenes. My team usually arrived at the battle site within an hour or two of the battle's end. The locale was always strewn with mortally wounded, already dead, and walking wounded. The stench of death was everywhere. I saw the bodies of 18, 19, and 20-year old American soldiers whose corpses had been mutilated by the enemy as a psychological warning.

I now believe that our nation has healed sufficiently so that a book of tragicomic tales from the Vietnam War can be printed. Amidst all of the blood, gore, and heartbreak, I saw some occasional humor in the events in which I had participated. Maybe this was my way of maintaining my sanity. I was fortunate as I was not generally in harm's way. However, the electronic intelligence community in Vietnam played a vital role in saving American lives. In many cases, we were able to forewarn U.S. commanders of impending Viet Cong and/or North Vietnamese military attacks. We were also able to give these commanders information on enemy locations, weaponry, tactics, and troop morale.

Thus, I ask readers to enjoy these tales in the light of the humor that can emerge from even the direst situations.

Peter J. Fournier
Raja & Associates
16807 Harrierridge Place
Lithia, FL 33547

Acknowledgments

First and foremost, I am grateful to my friend and editor, Julia Gabell, who worked tirelessly to compromise with me on the language and syntax of this project and who turned the other cheek when the text became bawdy and distasteful. And to the incomparable Sylvia Hemmerly, godmother to all aspiring authors, who guided me through the bewildering minefields of authoring and publishing.

I cannot fully express my gratitude to the people who encouraged me to embark on this project. Cathy Fournier, Michael Burton, John S. Burton, Michael Clabaugh, Stanley Jaffin, Joel Sherman, my sister Elaine and brother Paul were unflinching cheerleaders throughout this project. My heartfelt thanks also to Sharon Predham, my fiancée and emotional tower of strength who has stood by me—despite her doubts that a "humorous" book could ever be written about the Vietnam War.

For his clever and stunning jacket for my book, I want to thank George Foster. In my opinion, he is the maestro of intelligent and thought-provoking artistry. His ability to read my mind from his home in Iowa has stunned me.

My gratitude must also go to my publisher, Raja & Associates. Always available, day or night, when I needed them, their unselfish dedication to this project has been phenomenal and my dealings with them leave me with a "warm and fuzzy" feeling. They are an inspiration to me and to all others who have a story to tell.

And finally, in a book that occasionally highlights my exploits with women, I would be remiss if I did not mention one of the most extraordinary women I know. Lauretta Fournier, crossword puzzle addict, linguist, bridge player, Bourbon Manhattan aficionado, role model, and my sprightly 94-year-young mother, has touched my life in ways that I could never begin to express.

Chapter 1
February-May 1964

Fort Dix, the "Beginning"

America in the 1960s, dazed by the assassination of its youthful president, slid quickly from the promise of the preceding decade into the turmoil and positioning of political unrest. The world, once ordered and precise, now tottered on the brink of a fear and uncertainty that hung heavily over the grads from Millburn (NJ) High School. We had weathered the Cuban Missile Crisis and now a brush-fire war was evolving in Asia. No longer could we lounge within the glow of adolescent dreams, swaying to the strains of our Senior Prom or thrilling to the roar of cheering fans on the fields of athletic competition. The Cold War was on everyone's mind and a sense of uneasiness hovered all around us. The U.S. was beginning to send "advisors" to South Vietnam to help train the South Vietnamese Army to put down an emerging insurgency from internal (Viet Cong) and external (North Vietnam) forces.

Caught mid-stream in a swirl of teenage aspirations, I nevertheless felt the urgency of the hour. Kennedy had lit a torch (*". . . Ask what you can do for your country."*) and

Johnson had sounded the call. Service was no longer an option! Somehow throughout the years I had been bombarded with a sense of underlying patriotism that soon found me wedged uncomfortably in a long line of recruits filing nervously on the street outside the induction center at a Newark armory. Here, doctors would perform a cursory check for hernias and hemorrhoids and compile a five-minute medical history.

How had I arrived at this point in my life? I was ambivalent about what I was doing and where I was headed. My checkered post high school academic career had resulted in two ill-fated attempts to succeed at two different colleges. It did not take long for me to realize that my position as a lab assistant at Bell Telephone Labs was going nowhere fast. With the draft in full swing I was concerned that my number would come up very soon and I felt that, if I enlisted into the military, I might have a chance to control some of my fate.

I had heard that the Army offered the best chance for advancement, so I visited my local recruiter in Irvington, NJ. My intention was to find the "safest" military job available and to enlist for no longer than three years. The recruiter, however, piqued my interest with his glowing description of the many faraway places where I could be stationed and by listing the hundreds of opportunities available within the U.S. Army.

My first step was to take a general intelligence test to see if I was "Army materiel." On the day that I took the exam, the recruiter scored the results on the spot. I noticed that he kept going over and over the answer sheet and finally, after about twenty minutes, he called me over to his desk.

"Fournier, this is the highest score that I have seen in my five years as a recruiter. You literally have your choice of any specialty in the Army!"

I was stunned by his words, but I caught my breath and humorously replied, "O.K., Sergeant. If that's the case, I would like to begin at the top as a General."

The recruiter smiled, looked around the room, bent over close to my ear, and whispered, "Your score is too high!" We both cracked up laughing. At this moment, I knew that the Army had me.

In the conversations that I had had previously with the sergeant, he'd mentioned that linguists seemed to have the best duty. I remembered this, and because I was quite interested in languages, I asked him to tell me more about language opportunities. He informed me that I would first have to take the ALAT (Army Language Aptitude Test). He pulled a copy out of a drawer in his desk and he took me into a conference room attached to his storefront office.

"You've got one hour to complete this, Fournier, " I was told. "Then I will pick it up and grade it for you on the spot."

Seventy-five minutes later, he gave me the news. I had maxed the test! He proceeded to tell me that, if I signed up now, he could guarantee that I would be assigned to the West Coast Defense Language Institute upon completion of basic training. Later when I learned that I would be assigned to the language school in Monterey, California, I was thrilled.

"OK, Fournier, can't tell you just what language you'll be assigned—depends on the needs of the Army—but that's where you're heading: ol' 'Sunny Southern' . . . ."

Immediately I pictured white sand, surfboards, R&R on a pristine beach—and suddenly Army life looked golden!

The recruiter now outlined a new enlistment option that the Army had developed. I could join the Army Security Agency (ASA), an elite branch that dealt with intelligence issues, but one that was so secret that even he didn't know everything about it. He did advise me, however, that because ASA was so sophisticated and because the training was so technical and complex, the enlistment period was four years (the only four-year enlistment available in the Army).

He went on to tell me, "Fournier, you will be among the elite in the Army. Most of the members of ASA have some college and many of the enlisted men are college graduates."

I was dazzled by this appeal to my vanity and I hardly heard the words "four years." My hand trembled as I signed on the dotted line because I knew that I was changing my life forever.

When I informed my parents of my decision, they were elated. Now I would have a chance to "grow up" and get some direction in my life. As usual, they were right again. My mother was a fearful that I might have to fight in a war overseas, but Dad assured her that the action in Vietnam would be short-lived, and would be over by the time I finished basic training and my subsequent language training.

Thus, in February 1964, after a tearful round of goodbyes and fitful promises to write, I boarded a bus full of recruits headed from Newark to Ft. Dix. During the bus ride down the New Jersey Turnpike, I was in a heightened state of apprehension. The driver refused to answer any questions that his passengers asked him.

"You'll see when you get there," was all that he would say.

Not very comforting! After a two-hour bus ride we pulled into Ft. Dix. As we drove down the main road to our company area, soldiers wearing drab olive fatigues with white armbands shoveled gravel by the side of the road. A soldier carrying a rifle supervised them. I asked the driver what that was all about.

"Those are prisoners from the stockade," he warned. "That's what happens when you disobey your training sergeant."

"Oh shit," I thought to myself. *"What have I gotten myself into?"* Suddenly the thought of language school and sandy California beaches faded behind a dismal cloud of apprehension.

As we stepped from the bus into the center of the reception company area, a welcoming committee of training personnel surrounded us. Sharp orders punctuated the air.

"Stand over there!" "Stand over here!" Then "stand where you are!"

I was pushed and jostled and told to hurry up by the only person I can recall to this day: Sgt. Frank Bagnato. He was gruff, arrogant, and overbearing, an individual who just happened to be the Reception Company First Sergeant. Apparently he had earned a doctoral degree in "verbal harassment" and he made the most of his credentials.

"Keep moving," he screamed and, although I had my arms full with a civilian winter coat and a suitcase, I jumped in response to his command.

Finally we were herded into a rough formation in front of the dayroom and told to stand at attention. The cold, dreary February day seeped in to the very marrow of my bones.

For warmth I started to put my coat back on but was stopped dead in my tracks by Bagnato's shrill bark, "Did I tell you that you could move, recruit?"

"No, sir," I replied. The bitter weather seemed warm when compared to the cold fear I felt as I looked up into Bagnato's commanding eyes.

"I'm not a fucking 'Sir,'" he screamed, his twisted face about two inches from mine.

"I'm sorry, Sergeant," I gulped.

"You don't know how sorry you'll be if you ever call me 'Sir' again," he warned. I was totally intimidated by now and wanted only to get the hell out of there.

As we stood at attention, various members of the training staff introduced themselves and told us how much they "loved" us. We were to consider abuse and degradation as signs that they cared about us. I had never heard such perverted logic in my entire life.

We were then marched to our barracks, our main objective being to avoid stepping on the heel of the recruit in front of us. Our new quarters occupied the second floor, though bathroom facilities were on the first floor. As we ascended the stairs I caught a glimpse of twenty sinks backed by a wall of mirrors. About five feet in front of each sink there was a tank-type toilet beside which a roll of toilet paper rested on the floor. But I could not believe my eyes—there were no partitions between the toilets! Neither were there private shower stalls! The army had stripped us of any sense of privacy and a feeling of extreme dehumanization settled over me.

On the first full day of training we were herded over to a warehouse to be issued our fatigues, boots, gear, and weapons. Confusion reigned as 120 recruits grappled with their "stuff." At each clothing station stood a PFC who "estimated" your size. No need to argue; if the PFC said that you were a size 36, then you were a size 36. Later, when we got back to the barracks, we were able to swap clothing until everyone had uniforms that were approximately the right size. But nothing created quite so much interest as the dog tag stamping machine, a medieval device that looked like a typewriter with teeth. Operated by a Private who was waiting for his basic training cycle to begin, the clanging of the device captured our undivided attention as we stepped up to the table to be issued our tags.

The sergeant in charge was bellowing, "OK, scumbags, let's keep your fat asses moving! We're not on vacation here."

Were it not for the newness of the ordeal, it might have registered that we were truly being treated like "dogs" as we waited for our tags!

When it became my turn to step up, I announced loudly "FOURNIER! PETER J.! RA 12******!" And the Private dutifully pressed the appropriate keys to launch my dog tag creation.

"Religion?" he demanded, then awaited my response with an expression of complete disinterest.

The Devil made me do it! A rebellious wave swept over me and I blurted out," Orthodox Druid!"

"Spell that," he demanded.

"O-R-T-H-O-D-O-X space D-R-U-I-D," I spelled out with brutal emphasis. He kept tapping away, never catching on to my sarcasm.

The recruit behind me doubled over in laughter. "I would have figured you for Reformed," he quipped.

Attracted by our amusement, a take-charge drill sergeant stormed over to us and barked, "What the hell are you two maggots laughing about?"

Stopped short and caught in the throes of a joke we could not explain, we simply grinned in unison and replied, "Nothing, sergeant! Nothing at all!"

During the course of basic training, all new recruits were instructed in the use of the M-14 rifle. My company was one of the first to carry out marksmanship maneuvers using popup targets that were essentially silhouettes placed randomly in a landscaped field at a range of anywhere from 25 to 300 yards. As rifleman we were not only expected to *spot* these targets but were also expected to take aim and *hit* them. If someone scored, the target fell back down. As a young boy I had neither owned nor fired a gun of any kind, not even a Daisy or Red Rider Air BB Gun. I was, therefore, at a loss when I shouldered my first M-14 and sauntered out onto the firing range. I had one skill in my favor, however—my deadly accuracy with a slingshot, a flair honed during long hours of backyard squirrel chasing in suburban Short Hills.

In contrast, my training company included experts from Kentucky, West Virginia, and Pennsylvania who had been toting guns since they were toddlers. Each night in the barracks I listened as they bragged about the squirrels, birds, deer, raccoons, and groundhogs they had killed even before they'd gotten to first grade. Not comfortable input to quell the high apprehension level of a spoiled city boy!

On the first day of marksmanship training, I was singled out by the training staff.

"This guy's a 'virgin,'" remarked one marksmanship instructor as I stepped up to the firing line. "Let's give 'im all we got!"

I was not sure what this meant, but I certainly had no intention of questioning its source. But as soon as I heard the comment, I knew I was in for a run for my money. It was up to Fournier to LEARN or lose all face.

"Know how to 'true' your weapon, soldier?" I didn't.

"Well glue your eyes over here, son." It was during this phase that I learned to "true" my weapon just like everyone else, to synchronize my sight with the end of the barrel, and quickly "point and shoot." I shot from the standing position, the prone position, the squatting position, and from a foxhole. Each position required a different set of procedures and I found that I had learned them well.

I followed every direction that the training sergeant gave me and I "did it by the book." Moderately proficient, I simply did what I was told and asked questions as I went along. By the second week of marksmanship training I had gained a new level of confidence. I actually HIT most of the targets. Despite this, the thought of "qualifying day" shot nervous tremors up and down my spine. On this day a final determination would be made whether we were proficient enough to continue with basic training or whether we would be recycled (sent back for two additional weeks.)

I was a nervous wreck. Over and over I reviewed the various techniques that I'd been taught. *Oh well, maybe I'll be recycled right out of the Army!* In any case, I positioned myself on the firing line and braced myself for the onslaught.

"Stand and prepare to fire!" ordered the firing range Sergeant as he surveyed his potential line of apprentice warriors. "Ready on the left? Ready on the right? Commence firing!" he barked.

I looked out over the field, saw one target pop up, aimed, and fired. Ten successive minutes without pause and not a clue to indicate my score! We then repeated the sequence in a prone position, squatting stance, and from a foxhole.

At the completion of the firing I stood, my uniform drenched with nervous perspiration, my mind drained of all semblance of caring. Numbly I listened to the sergeant in charge as he droned on with the specifics.

"Gentlemen, your scores will be tallied and announced tomorrow morning at formation."

We were then herded onto trucks and driven back to the company area. Exhausted, I slumped onto my bunk and I left my fate in the hands of the US Army. At this point there wasn't a goddam thing I could do about it.

At formation the next day, the company was on pins and needles as the First Sergeant came out to speak to us.

"As a company, gentlemen, you've done very well indeed. Your scores are excellent, probably better than most groups we've had in recent months. No one from your group will be recycled."

A collective sigh of relief rose from the ranks.

"And now," he continued, "it is my pleasure to announce the name of the company sharpshooter, the soldier who came through the test with the highest score."

A visible stir rippled through those assembled in formation, each man secretly hoping to be the recipient of this coveted mark of respect.

"Private Fournier, front and center."

I almost fainted from surprise. Never had I expected to be the one singled out from the others, never had I imagined in my wildest dreams that my marksmanship would ever be recognized. I fell out of the formation, and approached the First Sergeant. He initiated the first salute and I smartly returned it.

"Private Fournier, you have made this company proud." So saying he pinned an Expert Medal (with M-14 bar) on my fatigue shirt and continued: "Furthermore, you have scored 995 out of a possible 1000 points, one of the highest scores that I have seen in my three years at Ft. Dix."

The grin on my face must have completely encircled my head as soldiers stared at me from every side. "Was *I* really this company's 'hot shot'?" Disparaging remarks from the disgruntled "hunters' in the unit simply rolled right past me and out into an empty void. No one could have stolen from me the thrill of this moment!

As if to rub salt in the wounds of those whose glory had been stolen, the First Sergeant further announced: "In special recognition of Private Fournier's accomplishment, I hereby exempt him from KP duty for the remaining four weeks of his basic training." The clouds parted and legions of Seraphim sang out for joy!

I later talked to officer friends about my surprising feat of marksmanship. Their response was that I had had no bad habits to break, and that the Army way of teaching marksmanship was tried and true. They felt that the experienced riflemen in the company were too proud to change. Sounds very logical to me!

One week before graduation from basic training we were given our new duty assignments. I was to report to the Defense Language Institute, Foreign Language Center (DLIFLC), in Monterey, California for a 47-week class in the Polish language. I was really happy because there were ominous signals coming from Vietnam that things might be getting hot. I seriously doubted that there would be a need for a Polish linguist in Vietnam. I graduated fifth in my class of 200 trainees. So far things were working out favorably. I went home for a two-week leave and to prepare mentally for my next duty station at the DLIFLC.

I had been home about a week when I received a phone call from some sergeant at the Army administrative center in Newark, NJ. He told me that my orders had been changed, "due to the needs of the Army." I was to report to Ft. Devens in Ayer, Massachusetts for training in Communications Traffic Analysis.

I told him that I already had orders to the DLIFLC. He told me that my orders had been changed and that I was to report to Ft. Devens or I would be considered AWOL. I called my recruiting sergeant in Irvington, NJ. His tone was quite different from when he was recruiting me to join the Army. He hardly remembered my name from three months previously. I asked him why my orders had been changed. He told me that the Army reserves the right to change any orders depending on their manpower needs. Apparently, someone somewhere had determined that Polish linguists were not a priority but Communications Traffic Analysts were. I was crushed. I thought briefly about going AWOL to Canada. I mentioned this possibility to my mother and father. Dad's reaction was typical: "You go; we don't know you."

My revised orders arrived by certified mail on the following day. I had seven days to get my head and emotions together. I finally realized that I should calm down because I had four years still ahead of me and fighting the system would be unproductive. Who knew what other opportunities might crop up? I would report to Ft. Devens, make the most of it, and see what happened.

Chapter 2
May-August 1964

Fort Devens

Uncle Gus waited anxiously at the Arrival Gate. His lopsided grin and the twinkle in his eye told me in no uncertain terms that he was as excited as I to be picking me up for my one-night stay at his home in Boston. Tomorrow he would drive me to Ayer where I would report to Fort Devens and my new assignment. I was beginning to look forward to what lay ahead. In the hectic wake of my last days at Fort Dix I slowly began to realize how lucky I was. I could have been assigned to A.I.T. (Advanced Infantry Training) after basic, where I would become a "ground-pounder" infantryman. But, here I was on my way to new experiences and challenges. My future was in THEIR hands!

My Uncle Gus was my father's younger brother who had served in the U.S. Navy during World War II. My father had received a critical industry deferment from military service because he worked for a major defense contractor. Gus's younger brother Emil had been rejected from military service for health reasons. At this time I was Gus's only relative who was performing military service and Gus was very proud of me. We talked until the early hours of the morning about his experiences in the Pacific during WWII. He gave me one very important piece of advice: "If you want to get along, go along." I had employed this philosophy during basic training and things had worked out well. Whether I could continue on this path was another story—my rebellious nature was probably too ingrained to overcome.

As our car wound along the manicured approach to Ft. Devens, my heart skipped a beat. The stately Georgian buildings loomed ahead, a tangible testimony to the great war effort of which I was now an integral part. For years Ft. Devens had been home to both an armored battalion and the United States Army Security Agency Training Center and School. Here Morse code intercept operators, cryptanalysts, traffic analysts, specialized equipment repairmen, and other related specialists were trained. Now I was going to take my place among the thousands who had preceded me, beside the men and women of military electronic intelligence. I had been assigned to learn Communications Traffic Analysis. This entailed taking intercepted radio communications "plain text" (already decoded by the cryptanalysts) and using the information to determine enemy unit strengths, locations, armaments, names of personnel, missions, radio call signs, communications networks, etc. The work sometimes resembled putting together a jigsaw puzzle or figuring a crossword puzzle.

"Over here, soldier! We'll check you in at the end desk." The booming voice of the soldier on duty bounced off the reception company walls.

It was not long before I had been duly processed and assigned to my barracks with other guys who would be taking the same class as I. As I left the building I suddenly felt the urgent need to use a latrine. A sign attached to the back of the stall door caught my attention: "PLEASE FLUSH TWICE, IT'S A LONG WAY TO THE MESS HALL." Was this an omen of things to come?

Apprehensively, I ambled over to the barracks and began to unpack my duffel bag. The pile of clothes on the top bunk indicated that another soldier had arrived before me. I had just begun to put my stuff away when a short, blonde, very self-assertive Private walked up to me.

"Hi, I'm Dave Dalton. I'm your roommate." I stuck out my hand to shake his. "Where you from, Fournier?"

"Jersey," I replied.

"Well, I'm a good old Philly boy who lost in the draft lottery. During my hernia check, I tried kissing the doctor on the head when he had his hand on my balls and told me to cough, but it didn't work. Look's like we're in this together!" He continued, "Even though my name tag says Dalton, I want to you recognize that my full name is David Patrick Lawrence Segrave-Dalton."

"What a little snot," I thought to myself. *"I don't know if we are going to last very long as roommates!"*

Life at Fort Devens proceeded with military precision. Each morning sleepy students stumbled into formation in front of the barracks then marched in step to class. Once in the classroom area we were told to fall out in order according to our assigned class. Communications Traffic Analysis was scheduled to last sixteen weeks. We attended class from 7:30 A.M. to 11:00 A.M. and then from noon to 4:00 P.M., Monday through Friday. Those not scheduled for weekend duty generally had time off with the stipulation to be back by 10:00 P.M. on Sunday. My courses were fairly easy and, much to my amazement, quite interesting. We learned early on that, by analyzing intercepted communications, one could decipher an incredible amount of information about the target.

As part of our military routine, we were expected to maintain our barracks in shipshape order. We were forced to suffer through regularly scheduled Thursday night "G.I. parties" where we were required to wash, wax, and buff the floors. I considered the entire exercise a complete waste of time, as did my good buddy Dave who shared my aversion and joined me in any ruse to avoid the hated activity.

Our luck changed about four weeks after our arrival when Dave discovered that those who attended college classes could be legitimately excused from G.I. parties. With escape in mind, we dashed over to the Base Education Office and found that we could enroll in courses at Boston University. With the new semester about to begin, we frantically searched through the evening catalog for *something, anything,* which met on a Thursday night. Lo and behold, there it was! BU was offering "History of the English Language" from 6 P.M. to 9:30 PM on Thursdays. With the required Army request form and BU paperwork in place, we raced back to the barracks to announce our academic aspirations. Three days later we were informed that we had both been approved and accepted. Annoyed that we had somehow beat the system, our barracks sergeant vowed that we make up the time in some other way.

During my first week of class, I also answered an advertisement in the Base newspaper for a 1960 Ford Crown Victoria. The soldier who owned it was shipping overseas and was eager to sell. For the mere sum of $750 I became the proud owner of a sleek, salmon-colored/white-topped sedan, a chrome-tipped beauty that, it turns out, became the perfect vehicle for our round trip to Boston University.

On the first night of class, Dave and I ate hurriedly and headed down Route 2 for the one-hour drive into Boston. We found our classroom and settled into our seats—three rows behind our barracks sergeant! He grinned roguishly when I waved to him and during our first class break, told us that he too hated the G.I. parties as much as we did. He thanked us profusely for "doing the research" that enabled him to find his *own* means of escape.

During the tenth week of classes at Devens, we were told that the unit was going to have a foot and wall locker inspection conducted by the post Commanding General. This was the first of the scheduled twice-yearly inspections carried out at every military post worldwide. Friday night witnessed a frantic cleanup. Everything had to be dusted, washed, waxed, spit shined, and in its place. We knocked off the cleaning at about midnight and rose early to put the finishing touches on everything. I was too busy to notice that one guy in the next cubicle wasn't doing any work in his space.

At the appointed time the inspection party entered the barracks. We all stood at attention in front of our footlockers, dressed in our best starched dress uniforms, and wearing our most highly polished low quarter shoes. The inspection party entered my area, examined both lockers, looked my cube mate and me up and down, and proceeded to the next cubicle. Suddenly, we heard a commotion.

"What's going on here, soldier?" the Commanding General snapped.

"I'm sorry, Sir. I just couldn't get started today," responded PFC Greco who was dressed only in a pair of olive drab boxer shorts and was sitting in the lower bunk munching Saltine crackers.

Someone gave the order to call the medics. Several minutes later, four soldiers showed up, stood by while Greco put on his clothes, and escorted him out of the barracks. Greco was literally taken away by "the men in white coats." Sunday morning, several soldiers I had never seen before arrived to pack Greco's belongings. They told me that he would be out of the Army by noon Monday on a mental disability discharge.

During the twelfth week of class we were asked to fill out a form (known as the Dream Sheet) on which we were allowed to request a new duty station upon graduation. I knew that this was a mere formality and probably an exercise in futility. The Army would send us wherever they wanted. On a lark, I requested one of the ASA installations in England, Germany, or Italy. Two weeks later, our new assignments came through. There were twenty-five men in my Traffic Analysis class. Twenty-three men received orders for various sites in Vietnam, one man received orders to Sinop, Turkey, and I was sent to Clark AFB, Philippines. I had no explanation for the distribution, but I do know that most of my classmates were angry that I seemed to have received some sort of special deal. I could only plead ignorance. I knew that my assignment was a two-year stint and I felt in my heart that I had dodged the Vietnam bullet. By the time my tour of duty in the P.I. was over, the small conflict in Vietnam would be resolved. I had, in essence, bought time.

The week before graduation, I sold my Ford Crown Victoria for $1000. The buyer had only $500 cash available, but assured me that his sister would send him the balance the following week and he would in forward it to me in the Philippines. I am still waiting! I estimate that, with interest, he now owes me over $60,000.

Chapter 3
December 1964

Welcome to Clark AFB

At the end of November 1964, I was assigned to the 9th USASAFS (United States Army Security Agency Field Station) at Clark Air Force Base. This was my first overseas assignment after graduating from Communications Traffic Analysis School. I was counting my lucky stars. The Philippines seemed like a cushy, straightforward assignment where all of the locals spoke English and actually liked Americans.

My first day was spent in-processing. I was assigned a room in the barracks and tossed my duffel bag on one of the beds. Although these were two-man rooms, when I first arrived I did not have a roommate. Each room had a desk, two beds, a large closet, and exited onto a balcony that extended the full length of the barracks. As an added feature, each room had a door that could be locked whenever the occupants left for the day. The doors and walls were louvered, allowing the air to flow freely, and an adjustable ceiling fan added to the over-all comfort. Even though the bathroom and showers were down the hall, I felt as if I were living in the lap of luxury. I could walk out onto the balcony and pick bananas, mangoes, and oranges from the overhanging trees. I truly thought that I had died and gone to heaven.

Once I checked into my quarters, my next stop was the personnel detachment. A personnel clerk took my orders and 201 File and introduced me to the Personnel Officer, CWO3 Grunion. Mr. Grunion asked to see my orders, then just stood there and stared.

After what seemed like an eternity, he looked down his glasses at me and asked, "What in the hell are you doing here, Fournier? We never asked Arlington Hall Station (HQ, ASA) for more personnel." I felt about six inches tall. He continued, "Well I guess, since we can't send you back, we'll have to keep you."

All I could do was smile weakly and mumble, "Good to be here, sir."

I walked slowly back to my room, sat dejectedly on the edge of my bed, and glanced over my in-processing checklist. It was only 3 P.M. so I still had time to report to the arms room. Gathering what little enthusiasm I had left, I returned to the main company area and asked the first person I saw for directions to the arms room. He pointed toward a building about fifty yards away.

From the counter at the front of the arms room, I could see someone rooting around in the back. I cleared my throat and a PFC emerged.

"What can I do for you?" he asked.

I responded that I was in-processing.

"OK, let's find you a weapon."

He took out a lined notebook and found an unassigned serial number and gun rack location. Again he went to the back room and returned with an M-16 rifle that he gingerly placed on the counter. The gun was filthy. I could see grit, spider webs, and a little rust forming in the barrel.

"This is your weapon," the PFC announced. I asked him if he had a cleaning kit that I could use right now.

"You won't need a kit, soldier. It's my job to keep your weapon clean."

"What! I don't have to maintain my own weapon?" I was totally dumbfounded by this new revelation.

"No, we do it all for you. And, the monthly cost is only $5.00." The PFC smiled smugly as he leaned against the counter and picked up the dirty weapon in front of him.

I was taken aback. "That's alright, PFC, I'll clean my weapon myself." No one else was going to maintain a weapon on which my life would depend.

"OK, if that's what you want to do. We're open for weapons cleaning on Saturday mornings from 7:00 to 8:00 A.M." He placed the rifle back down on the counter with an irreverent thud.

"You're shitting me," I replied. "Are those the only hours when the arms room is available?" I was beginning to harbor a very strong dislike of this guy.

"Well, do you want to join the club or not? You don't look like the type who wants to be the Lone Stranger. Take it or leave it. That's the schedule!"

When I said that I would think it over, he grabbed the M-16 and put it back in the gun rack. I stood there rooted in place and speechless for one of the few times in my life. I had never heard of such a setup.

The PFC returned and began to close up shop. "Hit the road, soldier. I'm through here for the day." I looked at my watch. It was only about 3:30 P.M.

"*Great job!*" I thought to myself. Then mentally I began to do some rough calculations. If I multiplied 400 Army guys by $5.00, the arms room was raking in approximately $2000 per month, a pretty decent piece of revenue for a job that cost this arrogant little PFC next to nothing. I knew damn well that the proceeds were being shared with the PFC, the SFC in charge of the arms room, the company 1st Sgt., the Executive Officer, and probably the Company Commander. Even being divided this many ways, it amounted to a nice piece of extra change.

The following morning, I took the company bus out to the Air Force Security Service (AFSS) and reported in to my new Section Chief, CWO4 Wetzel. (The AFSS had a large antenna field and were monitoring communications in Vietnam about 3,000 miles away).

Wetzel gave me a long quizzical look and barked, "What in the hell are you doing here? We're just biding our time until we move the whole operation lock, stock, and barrel to Phu Bai, Vietnam."

I gulped. "When are we moving?"

Visions of my cushy new assignment suddenly took on a dark and ominous tone.

"In sixty to ninety days," he replied. "Don't worry, Fournier. We don't have much to do. In the meantime, you'll be on the same schedule as everyone else in this section."

He noticed my puzzled look.

"You'll get the picture in just a moment, soldier," he said reassuringly. Wetzel continued his briefing.

"I want to see you here on Tuesdays, Wednesdays, and Thursdays no later than 10:00 A.M. We usually wrap it up by 2:00 P.M. I'll sign a four-day pass for you every week. Now, go get your picture taken for your security badge."

I saluted and walked briskly out the front door of the facility. I looked around. This remote section of Clark AFB could only be described as desolate. Since the next bus was not due for at least another half hour, I decided that I would start to walk and hitch a ride with the next vehicle that came down the road. Just then an airman emerged from the building, put on a motorcycle helmet, and revved a Lambretta motor scooter that was parked nearby.

"Want a ride, soldier?" he offered.

I climbed onto the seat behind him and we took off down the road. The air rushing by my face and the feeling of the open road unfurling beneath us gave me an indescribable high. Twenty minutes later we pulled up in front of my HQ building.

The driver introduced himself.

"Hey, by the way, I'm Airman Schultz."

The grin that spread across the face peering from behind the helmet said 'I'm your friend!'

"Glad to meet you! I'm PFC Fournier." I held out my hand to grip his warmly.

"Hey Fournier, can I buy you a beer?"

"Sure," I replied, already savoring the cool malt after a day of tense beginnings.

"Get back on."

Schultz accelerated out of the parking lot, turned right, and went about two hundred yards to the Clark

AFB Airman's Club. And to think this watering hole was only two hundred yards away from where I lived! I could see that there was also a small BX (Base Exchange) and liquor store attached to the Club.

On my first Saturday in the unit, I walked over to the arms room to clean my weapon. The PFC retrieved my weapon and handed me a cleaning kit. I sat on the floor and began to break down the gun for cleaning.

"How many other soldiers in the unit clean their own weapon?" I asked.

This looked as if it were going to be a very lonely occupation.

"You're a grand total of *one*," I was told.

By this time I was thoroughly disconcerted. I reached into my pocket and pulled out several bills.

"Here's your lousy fiver!" I growled as I forked over a bill.

He pulled out another lined notebook from under the counter. He wrote in my name and checked the paid column under 'December.'

"I guess it takes you all month to clean all four hundred of these weapons," I commented sarcastically.

I felt seconds away from a knockdown, drag-out fight, but I managed to maintain my cool.

"Are you kidding?" he sneered. "That's too much like work! I don't clean a weapon unless I absolutely have to. Let's just say that your $5 each month keeps you off the Old Man's shit list. You know, the 'List of Soldiers Who Didn't Clean Their Weapon This Month Report.' The Old Man likes to see a blank report. *Kapisch*?"

I walked out without saying a word.

That night, I went with four other guys to visit the base town of Angeles City, home of bars, nightclubs, brothels, restaurants, grocery stores, and anything else that you might desire. Angeles City was really the devil's home of every pimp and con man in the Philippines. This evening we decided to patronize the *Golden Eagle*, a favorite hot spot of my companions. The place was noisy, smoky, and the strippers were mediocre. By 1:00 A.M. we hailed a cab to take us back to the main gate at Clark, but on the way PFC Hammond insisted that we stop so that he could get something to eat. I joined him and the other two guys headed home. We had gone about half a block when we came across a Chinese carryout where each of us ordered a portion of pork-fried rice, an egg roll, and a Coca Cola. The rice and egg roll came wrapped in a piece of white paper whose corners had been crimped together to form a tent. As I unwrapped these items, I noticed that the paper was unusually thick and it had words typed across the sheet. And then I saw it! Neatly stamped on the top of the sheet were the words "Top Secret Kimbo." I accidentally dropped the entire rice-egg roll package onto the floor. I reached down and pulled out the soggy, greasy piece of paper. A closer look and I realized that what I had in my hand was an Air Force communiqué from the AFSS at Clark AFB to one of their units in Japan. I was so tired and hung over that I had trouble focusing on the text. I crumbled up the paper and put it in my pocket. PFC Hammond was so intent on eating that he never realized what had just happened. I had lost my appetite. I told Hammond to take his time and that I would meet him outside.

On Monday, I went over to the base G-2 (Intelligence) and turned in the crumpled paper. They refused to believe me when I told them where I had gotten it. The

Officer-in-Charge even intimated that perhaps I had stolen the document. In any case, they took a full report and told me to stay on the base in case they needed to talk to me further. I never heard another word from them. About a month later, I heard that an official Air Force investigation discovered that the restaurant was buying baled scrap paper from a Filipino trash subcontractor. Somehow a burn bag of classified trash had gotten mixed in with the day's regular trash. Several Air Force officers were quietly reassigned within the Far Eastern theater.

Chapter 4
December 1964–March 1965

The Extraordinary Tourist

As I described previously, when I reported for duty, Mr. Wetzel, the Section Chief, assured me that he would put me on the same schedule as the other personnel in the section. This meant that I would get a four-day pass every weekend. I thought, "What have I fallen into? Is this the Army? Or heaven?"

I decided immediately to take advantage of being in a foreign country friendly to the U.S. and to see as much of it as I could. I soon discovered that I could walk out the front gate of Clark AFB and catch a bus to Baguio City. This was the winter capital of the Philippine government and was located high in the cool mountains of northern Luzon. It was also the home of Camp John Hay, a U.S. Air Force R & R center and weather station. It was a good three-hour bus ride up steep mountain roads through the Philippine countryside. We passed through quaint villages like Pozzurubio, the home of Dr. Sanchez, apparently the most prominent doctor in town. The doctor lived in a palatial two-story all-mahogany house that had one very unusual feature. Attached to the roof and facing the road was a gigantic billboard (at least 25 feet wide by 10 feet high) with 6-foot letters that read, "DR. MANUEL SANCHEZ, M.D., TRAINED IN THE USA." Talk about outdoor advertising!

I could get a room for a couple of dollars per night at Camp John Hay and eat very well on the local economy. The weekend usually ended up costing me nothing because I used American cigarettes as "currency."

American cigarettes were rationed in the Philippines because Filipinos craved them. For example, a pack of Marlboros could bring 4 pesos ($1.00 US) on the black market. At the BX (Base Exchange) we were limited to six cartons of cigarettes per month. We all had ration cards that were punched each time we purchased cigarettes. At the time, a carton of American cigarettes cost $1.10. Since I was a heavy smoker, I bought my full allotment every month. Now the problem was to get the cigarettes off the base. The Air Police (AP) at the gate examined every suitcase, shopping bag, container, etc. that passed through. However, a friend of mine showed me the easiest way to smuggle cigarettes out. I put four packs in each sock and two packs in my underpants. When I was frisked by the Air Police, the cigarettes went undetected. The empty cardboard cigarette carton fitted neatly under the lining of my suitcase. When I arrived at Camp John Hay, it was very easy to re-construct a complete carton of American cigarettes. I always kept an open pack in my shirt pocket to bribe the cab driver that drove me out of the Camp. For two cigarettes he would signal the AP at the gate that I was "clean."

The first stop in Baguio was always the central market. Here cigarette vendors would vie for my cargo. I could sometimes get as much as $12.00 for a carton of cigarettes. This converted to about 48 pesos. A complete three-course meal with beer or wine at a nice restaurant would run about 4 pesos, while sandwiches or lighter fare would run about 1.5 pesos. Many times I was able to strike up a conversation with a local person in a restaurant and, when they found out that I was an American, I would end up not having to pay for my meal. All of the Filipino men wanted to tell me what they did during the Second World War and how they had been on General Douglas MacArthur's staff. If I had believed everyone, General MacArthur would have had a staff of 10,000. Anyway, on Sunday night I would discreetly count my money on the bus trip back to Clark. I usually had some pesos left over.

One might ask what I smoked since I had sold all of my cigarettes. Well, I didn't have to sacrifice too much. There was a local brand called Tabacalera that tasted very much like a strong Winston cigarette. They cost about 50 centavos (12.5¢ per pack) and weren't too bad once one got used to them. In fact, the tobacco in them was considered a premium blend of several Filipino tobaccos.

On one of my trips to Baguio, I had met an old Scotsman in a bar. He had run away to sea when he was fourteen years old and had jumped ship in Manila when the Captain found out his age and threatened to take him back home to his parents. He had survived somehow in Manila, married a local woman when he turned eighteen, and got a job with the Benguet Mining Company in Baguio. When I met Ian he was a foreman in the gold mines just outside Baguio. The two of us became fast friends and I always looked forward to meeting up with him. Ian once took me underground to see a working gold mine in operation. Unbelievable! He also liked to take me to the cockfights in a small town about twenty-five kilometers north of Baguio. We would sit in the cockfight stadium with several hundred local men and watch the fights. In the stands, the betting was always fast and furious. I even won 100 pesos one evening! Ian told me that three Lebanese brothers who had purchased their best breeding birds from Texas controlled the entire cockfighting industry. Ian really was a good friend and confidante. One day as we were walking along the sidewalk, I was approached by a dark pregnant Filipino woman who began to touch my arms, shoulders, and face. I immediately recoiled and pushed her away because I thought that she was trying to pickpocket me. Ian intervened and apologized to the woman. He explained to me that the women merely wanted to touch me in hopes that her baby would be born light-skinned.

During this time I also spent a good deal of time at *The Rice Bowl Restaurant*, headquarters of the Baguio Chess Club. There were about twenty tables for eating, and each of them had a complete chessboard inlaid into the tabletop. Chess matches went on day and night. At any one time there must have been ten games in progress. I used to stand and watch with other enthusiastic spectators. I was always invited to sit and play, but I really never seriously cared for the game of chess. However, I could usually find a bridge game in one of the local social clubs.

It was also during this time that I discovered the "deal of deals." A gentleman that I met on the bus to Baguio told me that the Philippine Airlines had a year-round special of anywhere in the Islands for 100 pesos ($25.00 US). The only catch was that the planes were cargo planes that had only one or two sling type mesh seats available on each flight. Additionally, the planes would depart from the Manila International Airport freight terminal at all hours of the day or night. The fun was to show up and see what was going where. I took flights that departed at 3 A.M. and 3 P.M., at 5 A.M. and 5 P.M., at midnight and at noon. I would just pack a soft carry-on bag, a bagged lunch, and come to the terminal prepared for any eventuality. Since I had four days off every weekend, the possibilities were unlimited. I soon befriended the scheduler and he would recommend certain destinations to me. During my four months in the Philippines, I managed to see Iloilo, Palawan, Negros Occidental, Zamboanga, and other exciting destinations. Some of the flights lasted eight to ten hours with one or two stops in between. I would ride backwards in one of the sling seats and just relax. All of the pilots got to know me and treated me like a celebrity. They all wanted to know how they could join the U.S. Air Force or become American commercial pilots. I told them that I would find out and get back to them. Of course, I didn't have a clue as to what I needed to do to get them their information. I kept saying that their best bet was to contact the U.S. Embassy in Manila. I hoped that I was right!

When we arrived at our destination, I always took a taxi to the central market of the nearest large city. Here I could get information on available lodging and the best places to eat. In many cases, the people had not seen a Caucasian in many years and I became quite a curiosity. I had managed to learn some "touristy" Tagalog (the official language of the Philippines) and that enhanced my reputation even more.

I can recall one especially pleasing excursion. I caught a flight from Manila to Tuguegarao, located in the far northeast corner of the island of Luzon (where Clark AFB was located). It was approximately a two-hour flight over very high mountains. When we arrived, I took a taxi into town, as was my habit. I headed straight for the central market. I began to wander among the stalls of fruits, vegetables, artwork, handicrafts, etc. I had stopped to look at some paintings done on velvet when I was aware of someone standing directly behind me. I wheeled around and looked straight into the eyes of a gorgeous Caucasian, blue-eyed, blond-haired, and svelte female.

She smiled lasciviously and asked, "Are you an American?"

I was totally overwhelmed, not only by her beauty but also by her assertiveness. Absolutely the last thing I ever expected was to encounter a Caucasian woman in such a remote area.

"Sure am," I replied weakly.

"Boy, am I glad to see you!" she retorted.

I am sure that I looked very puzzled to her. She took my hand and started to lead me away. I feigned resistance.

She gave me an order, "Let's go have a drink."

Immediately, my eyes undressed her and I became aroused. However, I wanted to "stay cool" and not let her know that I was now "hot" for her body.

"OK, OK," I said. We sat down at an outdoor café and ordered two bottles of San Miguel beer.

"Hi, my name's Pete. What are you doing here?"

I found that I was now fumbling to make intelligent conversation. She had me under her spell and I loved every minute of it.

She smiled seductively.

"I'm Elizabeth but you can call me Lolita. I'm here with the Peace Corps and you're the first American I've seen in eight months."

"Eight months? Wow, you must be really homesick!"

"Not homesick, stupid. Horny!"

I grinned from ear to ear and replied, "Lolita, today is your lucky day. I think that I can help."

I had recovered my composure and I would now be able to take full advantage of the situation.

"I do, too," she coyly replied.

We made love with our eyes, paid, and left the café. The beer had gone directly to my head and I was now totally relaxed in her presence. We walked down the street to a large dirt parking lot. Lolita owned a jeep and we jumped in with her at the wheel. She took off down a narrow dirt road away from town. About ten minutes later we arrived at a thatch-roofed nipa hut on stilts. Pigs, ducks, and dogs scurried around the grounds. Lolita took me up the ladder and into her hut. She had a Coleman stove, a small refrigerator that ran on butane, a bed with a straw mattress, and a bureau. I asked her about a bathroom. She informed me that it was out back in the bushes. Before I could even get my bearings, Lolita had already removed her blouse and shorts and was standing there wearing only her bra and panties.

"I don't have any condoms with me."

"I won't tell if you don't," she replied. She began to unbutton my shirt. The rest will go untold. . . .

All I can say is "SPECTACULAR!" I found out that Lolita was a civil engineer who had graduated from Cal Tech. She was working with the local authorities to design and implement a safe drinking water system for the town. In her spare time Lolita taught English classes at a local elementary school, and directed the church choir where she worshipped. I felt humbled in her presence because she was so beautiful and so brainy. Somehow, I managed to get back to Tuguegarao three more times for long weekends, twice by Philippine Airlines and once by bus.

We corresponded for about a year, but she eventually fell in love with her Peace Corps Country Chief and married him. Lucky guy!

Chapter 5
January 1965

Medical Embarrassment

As mentioned, the base town of Angeles City was a thriving town with a whorehouse on every corner and prostitutes who worked the bars. It was no wonder that venereal disease (mostly non-specific urethritis or gonorrhea, both known as "the clap") was a constant threat to GIs and Air Force personnel. Our officers and senior enlisted men formally counseled us to use a condom, but generally the words fell on deaf ears. "I don't wear a raincoat when I take a shower" was the prevailing attitude.

One day I was in the barracks men's room when I became conscious of a member of my unit using the urinal next to me. He was gripping the cold water inlet pipe with both hands and was in obvious pain as he started to urinate.

"That piece of ass I had last week was so good I'm still coming," he exclaimed. "Gotta see Borja!"

I laughed out loud.

"Who's Borja?" I asked.

I imagined that Borja was some Filipino venereal disease oracle whose magical potions protected all GIs.

"He's the clap doctor over at the hospital."

This concept was unusual to me. While I was at Ft. Devens, I learned that soldiers contracting venereal disease were considered mentally unstable by the Army and were usually referred to a psychiatrist for counseling. However, at Clark AFB the military seemed to have a more "enlightened" and "realistic" attitude about venereal disease and made condoms widely available, usually placing a cartridge magazine case of condoms and a large warning sign next to the sign-out book in the orderly room. Contracting VD was now considered just another medical problem, easily treated with procaine penicillin and tetracycline. However, I was also aware of disciplinary action being taken against individuals who contracted VD multiple times.

"Oh, I hope that I never meet him." I replied.

The thought of having to deal with such problems hadn't quite settled in as yet.

"If you stay here long enough, you will," he said with a wink through gritted teeth.

I could see that he was in considerable pain. At this point I made a promise to myself to be ultra careful so that I would never have to go through what he was experiencing.

Several weeks later I met Josephine, a cute little Filipino waitress in a restaurant in Angeles City. We hit it off immediately. Josie spoke good English and could carry on a moderately intelligent conversation. We began to date and I would take Josie with me to Baguio City in the mountains on weekends when she could get off work.

Josie had her own one-bedroom efficiency above a dry cleaning establishment owned by her brother. Many nights after Josie finished her shift at the restaurant, we adjourned to her place for drinks and sex. Josie liked to be kittenish. She had a large closet at the foot of the bed with a curtain over the opening. There she liked to slowly undress and then drape herself with the curtain while she performed a sexy striptease. She really knew how to turn me on! Josie was my only sexual partner during those days.

One morning, I got out of my bunk in the barracks and stumbled down to the bathroom. I was immediately aware of a burning sensation when I urinated, but figured that the processed beer from the night before probably caused it. As the day went on, however, I noticed an increased burning sensation accompanied by a light-yellow stain in my underwear. I was highly agitated because Josie and I seemed to be an exclusive. She had even proposed marriage to me; an idea I had cleverly declined by saying that the Army wouldn't let soldiers of my rank get married. In any case, I now decided it was time to go on sick call at the hospital.

That afternoon I went to the base hospital and signed in at the emergency room. A nurse took my vitals and asked me about my complaint.

When I described the problem, she said mockingly, "You need to see Dr. Borja! Go down to Room 100 and wait outside."

I walked down the hall and sat on a padded bench placed against the wall outside Room 100. The nurse followed several minutes later with my medical records and disappeared into Room 100 for about ten minutes. She emerged and gave me a knowing smile as she walked back to the emergency room. I looked around. The Obstetrics/

Gynecology Department, the Pediatrics Department, and the Laboratory were all within twenty-five yards of where I was waiting. I could see pregnant women sitting on benches and screaming kids running up and down the hallway.

The door to Room 100 opened and a grandfatherly man invited me in. He pointed to a chair next to his desk. Apprehensively I sat down.

"I am Dr. Borja," he said as he put out his hand. "What seems to be the problem?"

Without waiting for an answer, he motioned for me to drop my pants.

I stood there lamely with my pants around my ankles and told him about the burning and the pus. He took a glass microscope slide from a credenza next to his desk and handed it to me.

"Here, milk some pus onto this for me." I obeyed and handed the slide back to him.

He then told me to pull up my pants and he left the room. A few minutes later Dr. Borja returned.

"Just wanted to drop the slide off at the lab," he informed me. "Now, let's have a look in my book."

Dr. Borja produced a three-ring binder containing many photographs of young women. He explained that these were pictures of prostitutes taken by the Angeles City Health Department when these women came in for their semi-annual venereal disease inspections. (Prostitution was not legal but was tolerated in Angeles City). Dr. Borja told me that women could actually become "licensed" by the city. He asked me to look through the photos and see if I could pick out the woman who probably gave me my problem. I leafed through the pages one by one. None of the women looked familiar. While I examined the pictures, Dr. Borja explained to me that he was a Filipino M.D. trained in the U.S. and that he was the hospital's one-man "Venereal Disease Department." Well, at least I was being treated by a specialist! Dr. Borja told me to wait outside until the lab results came back. It would take about thirty minutes.

I went outside and sat on the padded bench. I was soon joined by three airmen who were experiencing difficulties similar to mine. Dr. Borja saw them one by one. An hour had elapsed when someone from the lab knocked and then entered Room 100. One minute later Dr. Borja came out into the hallway. He had my medical records in his hand. He took one step toward me, looked me straight in the eye, and turned to face down the hallway.

At the top of his lungs he screamed, "Private First Class Fournier, you have the clap!"

He turned 180 degrees and faced down that hallway.

Again he screamed, "Private First Class Fournier, you have the clap!"

He handed me my medical records and a drug prescription, and then retreated back into Room 100 closing the door behind him. I looked around. All of the pregnant women were staring at me and giggling among themselves.

One of the women echoed, "Fournier, you have the clap!"

Dr. Borja's booming voice had scared some of the children and they began to scream and cry.

A nurse walked by, laughed, and said, "It must be Borja time!"

I was beside myself. I sat as if glued to the bench. My knees refused to work. I finally mustered the strength to get up. I put my baseball cap and medical records folder over my face and tried to navigate toward the front exit. As I hastily walked toward "freedom," people pointed and laughed. I had never been so humiliated in my life. When I got to the front door, I took off running. The catcalls and booing still rang in my ears.

Later that day, I asked a friend of mine to drop off the prescription for tetracycline at the hospital pharmacy. I waited three days and then went and picked it up myself. I was also given an information sheet of the "Do's and Don'ts" to follow while under treatment. When I got back to the barracks, I looked the sheet over. Item #1 said, "When you urinate (*take a piss*), always remember . . ." Just like the military, forever catering to the lowest common denominator by defining the obvious.

Chapter 6
March 1965

Military Surgery

All of the operational personnel in the 9th USASAFS were required to hold Top Secret clearances. We had to be careful to whom we spoke, what we revealed, what we did, how we did it, why we did it, and to whom it was directed. We were constantly urged to minimize close contact with foreign nationals and, in most cases, were prohibited from co-habiting with any of the local women. This was fairly universal throughout the Army Security Agency (ASA) worldwide. At many ASA outposts, there were detachments of Criminal Investigation Command (CID). These guys wore civilian clothes and were the local military gumshoes. If there were suspicions that an ASA enlisted man was living with a local girl, the CID would be assigned to tail him and verify the hunch for his superiors.

Because of the nature of our business and security clearances, whenever a member of the 9th was scheduled for surgery under general anesthesia, another member of the unit had to be present to ensure that the patient didn't inadvertently mumble something classified. The

Company clerk was responsible for maintaining a duty roster for this purpose. As luck would have it, my name came up shortly after my arrival. I checked with the Company clerk and he told me that I was assigned to be present at surgery for SP5 Mulcahy at the Clark AFB Hospital on a particular day and time. I was to report to the Outpatient Surgery desk.

I reported as ordered and was shown to a room where I was given a green surgical gown, cap, and shoe covers. I was told to go to Room 206 and wait for further orders. When I arrived, I saw a person lying face down and naked on a gurney at the back of the room. A sheet was covering his legs and feet from just below his buttocks.

I said, "Hi, I'm Pete Fournier. Mulcahy, I presume?"

"Yup," came the response.

His one-syllable response sounded so forlorn that I couldn't help but feel immediate empathy with him.

"What are you in for?" I asked.

"A circumcision," he replied with obvious dread and uncertainty in his tone.

"Are you serious?"

This was such an unexpected answer that I found it hard to respond to the situation that was both embarrassing for me and stressful for him.

"Yep, got some sort of problem with my dick."

Obviously, this was a serious problem if he was being prepped for surgery under general anesthesia.

At this moment an individual dressed for surgery and pushing a prep cart entered the room and approached the gurney.

"I'm Captain Fleisher. I'm the anesthesiologist on this case."

He reached out his gloved hand and shook my hand. I found it strange that he did not shake hands with Mulcahy. He looked down at the person on the gurney.

"You Mulcahy?"

"Yes sir."

The more Mulcahy made an effort to project his voice, the farther he seemed to sink into the oblivion of the white sheet that covered him.

"OK, there's been a change. I'm going to give you a saddle block. It will only hurt momentarily, so buck up!"

Captain Fleisher took an alcohol swab and wiped the base of Mulcahy's spine. He next took a ballpoint pen from his pocket and proceeded to draw three concentric circles at the cleansed site. My eyes got bigger and bigger as I realized what had just happened. FLEISHER HAD DRAWN A TARGET! He took a large syringe from the prep cart, held it about ¾" above the "bulls eye," and "fired." The syringe went straight to the mark. Mulcahy let out a muffled scream. I sat down on a nearby stool so that I wouldn't fall far when I fainted. I looked away.

"There, that should do it. I'll be back in fifteen to twenty minutes."

Captain Fleisher exited the room. I wheeled myself on the stool toward the gurney. Mulcahy's complexion was as white as the sheet that covered his legs.

"Hey, how are you doing?" I asked.

Never in my life had I seen anything to equal this display of medical marksmanship!

"Man, if I ever see that son-of-a-bitch on the street, I'll kill him."

Mulcahy tried bravely to fight the pain, but I knew he was chewing bullets.

"I'll help you!" I promised.

And at this point I really meant it.

True to his word, Captain Fleisher returned in fifteen minutes. He began to pinch Mulcahy on the calves, hips, and back.

"Can you feel that?"

Mulcahy replied, "Yes sir."

"OK, we'll wait a couple of minutes more."

Fleisher went over to the window and stared outside. As if he were without a care in the world, he nonchalantly began to softly whistle "Camptown Races."

About five minutes later, Fleisher tried the "pinch test" again. Again, Mulcahy responded that he could still feel the pinching. Announcing that time was of an essence and that we couldn't wait any longer, Fleischer assured Mulcahy that the anesthesia would take hold by the time they were ready in the OR. He began to push the gurney toward the door and instructed me to follow. We went down several halls and entered Operating Room #3. Mulcahy was transferred to the OR table, draped so that only his penis was visible, and told to relax. The surgeon now entered the room. I couldn't believe my eyes— a lady surgeon! She was ready to begin when she noticed me.

"Who are you?" she asked.

Prepped and set for business, she left not a doubt in the world that she *meant business*.

"I'm SP4 Fournier from this guy's unit. I'm here to do whatever needs to be done if he starts talking. We have high clearances."

As important as that may have sounded to me and to the men in my unit, it was obvious that this lady was not one bit impressed. She scowled.

"Incidentally, what do I do?" I inquired.

"Here, hit him with this!"

From somewhere on the table behind her she produced a stainless steel hammer, something that an orthopedist might use with his stainless steel chisel. She handed the hammer to me. I stood riveted to the spot— a stone presence, mouth open and speechless. I didn't know "whether to shit or go blind." My eyes seemed to be darting, in a triangular pattern. The hammer, Mulcahy, the surgeon, the hammer, Mulcahy, the surgeon.

Fleisher was still trying to confirm that Mulcahy was now sufficiently desensitized by the anesthesia. It appeared that all was a GO! I took several steps backward so that I was now behind the three-person surgical team: the surgeon, the anesthesiologist, and an airman nurse. I sat on a stool, but I could still see everything that was going on. Mulcahy had a large green drape suspended in front of his face so that he could <u>not</u> see what was going on. The surgeon began to cut. She was about half of the way around the foreskin on Mulcahy's penis when Mulcahy let out a blood curdling scream!

"Jesus Christ, what the fuck are you doing?" he screamed.

He jerked up and down on the OR table, pulling at the restraining straps.

The surgeon's face turned red and she embarrassingly said, "Sorry, soldier. I guess you weren't completely numb!"

"No shit," Mulcahy replied.

I heard the surgeon say "Local".

At this point a large syringe with a six-inch needle appeared. I gasped as the surgeon plunged the syringe into the shaft of Mulcahy's penis. And then I fainted dead away!!

I awoke in a recliner chair in the recovery room.

A nurse walked up to me and announced, "You can go now. Mulcahy's going to be alright."

I looked around. Mulcahy was sound asleep in a bed nearby. I got up, took off my surgical paraphernalia, and quickly exited the room. As I walked outside, a steady rain began to fall. I had taken half a dozen or so steps when it hit me squarely in the gut. I didn't even need to be there! Mulcahy's surgery had been performed under *local* anesthesia!

Goddam it, they had screwed me again!

I half-walked, half-jogged the entire two miles back to the Company area in the rain, staunchly refusing three ride offers from passing cars. Only a long cold trek along muddy roads in the drenching rain could possibly wash away the residue of what could only be called "one hell of a day"! I had been a participant in a surreal drama, a time in space, that, to this day, I still cannot fully comprehend.

Chapter 7
April 1965–April 1966

Language on Vacation

One day in the middle of March, 1965, I happened to notice an announcement on the company bulletin board. In large lettering it read:

> "URGENTLY NEEDED. Personnel SP4 and above needed to study the Vietnamese language at Fort Meade, MD. Application must be received by Arlington Hall Station no later than March 18, 1967."

I was immediately interested. I read the ten required qualifications, and realized that I unfortunately met only three. I also realized that the deadline for applications was just three days away. Despite these potential obstacles, I spoke with my First Sergeant about this opportunity and he encouraged me to apply anyway. I rushed over to the ASA personnel building and asked to speak with CWO3 Grunion, the man-in-charge. He was a grizzled old guy who had come up through the ranks from Private to Chief Warrant Officer. He invited me into his office and I explained my dilemma, emphasizing that I only met three of the announcement criteria but that I really wanted to go. He kept reading and rereading the announcement and looking up at me. He was thinking so intensely I could almost smell wood burning. He finally put the notice down, looked straight into my face, and pointed his finger at me.

With an air of authority he announced, "Don't you realize, soldier, that ANYTHING in the Army can be waived? If I decide that you should go, you'll go!"

I was very impressed.

"How badly do you want this?" he asked.

"Very badly, sir. I think that I can make a valuable contribution to the mission of the United States Army."

Grunion had tossed a few crumbs of hope and I was willing to gather them up.

"Cut the bullshit," he demanded as he handed me an application to fill out.

Obviously the man was a no-nonsense, self-made type of guy. Suddenly, I found myself looking at him with a newfound respect.

"What about the deadline?" I asked.

No matter how excited I was, there were still practical considerations to take into account.

"Don't get your balls in an uproar. Just have this back to me this afternoon," he ordered.

He pushed back from his desk and looked me squarely in the eyes.

"Get your ass moving, soldier!"

"Yessir!"

I took the application, ran back to the barracks, and poured over every word on every page. Within fifteen minutes I had it completely filled out and raced back to Personnel. I could tell Grunion was impressed.

"My God, Fournier, you really *do* want this assignment! O.K. We'll get it moving! Hang tight and check back with me in ten days."

Five days later I was told that Personnel wanted to see me. I literally flew over on a cloud of enthusiasm. Mister Grunion came out of his office and handed me a thick packet of documents.

"Congratulations, soldier. You're going to Fort Meade."

I was so excited that I almost fainted.

"You're pulling my leg. Right, sir?"

As much as I wanted to believe that my good fortune was a reality, I held back. Too often I had stepped up to the plate, only to swing futilely at one of life's fastballs.

"I suggest that you start out-processing immediately, Fournier, because you leave in three days."

Though gruff and to the point, I could tell his warning was couched in a certain satisfaction. He was actually happy for me and pleased with himself for making it happen.

Later that day, the Company Commander told me that he had never seen such efficiency in his twenty years in the Army. My paperwork had gone from Clark AFB to Camp Zama, Japan to Arlington Hall Station, Virginia and back in four days—a new world's record! In any other situation we were talking a minimum of four to six weeks.

I had dodged another Vietnam bullet. Another year would elapse before I finished language school and by then the small police action in Vietnam would surely be over. I hopped on my motor scooter and headed for the base chapel. With a sigh of relief I knelt in one of the pews and thanked the entire pantheon of saints, cherubs, and spirits that make up the Christian faith.

Three days later I was seated on a plane headed back to the United States. Two days after landing, I arrived at Ft. Meade, and in-processed to my new unit. I was to be a student at the National Cryptologic School run by the National Security Agency, a school that also provided training in many of the other skills needed by employees of the Agency. On the first day of class, I noticed that there were civilians as well as military personnel in our classrooms. Starting at the same time as my forty-seven-week class were courses in "Special" Arabic, Serbo-Croatian, and Mandarin Chinese. The "Special" Arabic class was made up entirely of Navy personnel, the Serbo-Croatian class was all civilian, and the Mandarin Chinese class was 75/25 female. I got to know several of the Navy enlistees during class breaks and finally had an opportunity to ask what "Special" Arabic meant. Because what they were doing was classified, they couldn't tell me, but one Navy buddy did say that at graduation he would probably be fitted for a yarmulke. I later pieced this information together and figured that the U.S. Navy ships steaming around in the Mediterranean were apparently intercepting Israeli communications and needed Hebrew linguists to do translation.

My classmates and I attended class from 8:00 A.M. to noon and from 1:00 P.M. to 4:00 P.M., Monday through Saturday. The grueling schedule gave us facility in reading, writing, and speaking another language using combinations of written and spoken communication. We had homework every night and I was convinced that I would end up with cauliflower ears because I spent so much time glued to earphones in the language lab. Our team of three instructors drilled us relentlessly. Weekly written and oral tests kept us buried in books and wired into high-pressure mode. Each month we could expect a barrage of written tests followed by oral exams that lasted a minimum of three hours each. By the end of my first three months I swore that my eyes had begun to slant!

Our total immersion in the Vietnamese language was pushed to the limit. Once we passed through the chain-link fence that surrounded our barracks, English was positively forbidden. There was a branch of the base PX and a barbershop within the compound and even there all transactions were conducted in the Vietnamese language.

Each day we read *Nhan Dan,* the morning newspaper from Hanoi. Air France ran two daily flights from Paris to Hanoi during the entire Vietnam War. When the plane was refueling in Hanoi for its return trip, newspapers were loaded onto the plane for delivery to the large North Vietnamese community living in Paris at the time. Of course, a number of copies were commandeered by someone in Paris and were forwarded to the United States. Amazingly, our copies of *Nhan Dan* were only two days old when we received them. We would then read about how the loyal, patriotic North Vietnamese Army (NVA) had shot down 5,000 U.S. planes, destroyed 10,000 U.S. tanks, and killed 25,000 U.S. soldiers during a battle three days ago. If you added everything up, we must have had five million soldiers in Vietnam at any one time. The Army of the Republic of South Vietnam (ARVN) was characterized as "puppets of the aggressive American imperialists." The editors of *Nhan Dan* didn't realize it at the time, but they were essentially publishing a daily humor magazine.

I remember one very interesting front-page article. There was a picture of Ho Chi Minh pinning a Heroes Medal onto the pajama top of a local peasant. The accompanying article explained that this peasant was the "Provincial Feces Champion." In other words, this peasant had personally produced more human fertilizer than anyone else in the province during the previous twelve months. I was quite impressed. Even some people whom I considered to be "full of shit" could never hope to hold a candle to this guy! I wanted to make a large poster out of the photograph and story, but I was told that it might offend our instructors because I would be making fun of their culture.

About three months later, a large headline in *Nhan Dan* announced: "Peasant Executed for Fraud." As we read further, it became clear that this peasant was our friend, the "Provincial Feces Champion." Apparently, the authorities had discovered that this peasant was mixing his feces with straw and small rocks before bagging it and taking it to the weighing station. He got caught red-handed. Justice was swift. The local citizens' revolutionary council had tried, convicted, and executed this poor man within twenty-four hours of the original charges brought against him.

At the end of forty-seven weeks we were told that we now had a working vocabulary of 5,000 Vietnamese words. Amazingly, the average native speaker has a working vocabulary of only 2,500 words. I graduated first in the class and was given a Certificate of Achievement. The Director of the National Cryptologic School came to our graduation and, after the ceremony, introduced us to a General Underwood. We were asked to sit down and General Underwood came to the podium. I noticed that the doors to the auditorium were being closed and that there were numerous MPs milling around. The General introduced himself and told us that he had a very important Top Secret announcement. He told us that, as special students, the twenty of us had been "hand picked" to accompany U.S. troops during a massive invasion of North Vietnam to take place within the next three to six months.

My knees suddenly went weak and I began to wonder what *hari-kari* would be like. "A massive invasion of North Vietnam!" Holy shit! I could feel my pulse beginning to race. I now knew why we had studied aerial maps of Hanoi, Haiphong, and other Northern cities. I now knew why we were taught the Northern dialect exclusively. I now knew why we had studied Northern culture and Buddhist philosophy. I now knew why we had even learned about Northern cuisine and dietary habits.

I suppose if you have to die, you might as well die prepared. I looked around at my classmates. Most of them stared dead ahead in a trance-like state. Not one word was exchanged. I elbowed the guy next to me in the ribs, but he didn't budge. After five minutes of stunned silence, we filed out of the room like stoned zombies headed to face the daunting prospect of new and unfamiliar worlds.

Chapter 8
April 1966

Who's On Third?

The Pan American contract flight banked sharply as it headed in for a landing at Ton Son Nhut Airport. As far as the eye could see, a large checkerboard of rice paddies separated by ribbons of water fanned out before us. In random squares one could also see the dense jungle canopy. No roads, no buildings, no people. Only dark green, dense foliage—and the vague skyline of Saigon on the far horizon.

The ten-hour flight from Honolulu had been long, broken only by occasional announcements from the cockpit or trips down the narrow aisle to stretch one's cramping legs or relieve a nagging bladder. No one pretended to know the real reason for our flight into this unknown land. Rather, homesick and frightened, we fell silent as we gawked through the narrow windows at the ground 2000 feet below.

"This is the Captain speaking. We are preparing to land at Ton Son Nhut. . . ."

At the Captain's announcement, every soldier sat up and took notice. Saigon! We craned our necks in a last desperate effort to catch the first glimpse of life in a place that would be our home for the next 11 months and 25 days. From this point on, I knew my life would change.

On the morning after my arrival, we "newbies" were asked to line up in front of the orderly room to receive our duty assignments. SFC Pribble took attendance and instructed us to yell "Here, Sir!" when he called our name. My mood was dark and rebellious. I hated the war. I hated the Army. And I maybe even hated myself. I heard Pribble bark "Fournier!" A latent devil lurking deep within me leapt out.

"*Ici*, I mean *HERE*," I responded.

The look on the Sergeant's face froze and for a split second I thought that I had just bought a third class ticket out of the Army and into the brig.

"Excuse me, Specialist Fournier. Did I hear you say *Ici*?"

My knees started to sag. *Why did I have to be such a colossal bad ass?*

"*Oui*," I answered weakly.

"Fournier, eh," he inquired. "That's a French name, right?"

He stood directly in front of me as I held my breath and tried desperately to keep up a brave front.

"French-Canadian," I corrected him, though I now was very aware that I'd better make a 'best friend' of this guy.

"Well, I'll be a son-of-a-bitch! I think we've got our French 'lingy!'" he chuckled.

"I don't understand, Sarge."

I had no idea what Pribble was talking about. I just stood in place, staring straight ahead and hoping that whatever I had or hadn't done wouldn't come back to haunt me.

"See me after this formation, Fournier," he barked.

He proceeded to tell us that we were to be at the main gate at 7:30 A.M. to catch the bus to Operations at White Birch. The group began to disperse and I turned and took several steps away from where Pribble was standing.

I heard him scream, "Fournier, get you fat ass over here now!"

I wheeled about face and walked up to him.

"What's going on? What do you want with me?" I asked.

I was annoyed and confused by this small chain of events.

"Fournier, are you familiar with the term 'needs of the Army'?"

Two eyes set in his ruddy face bore directly into mine.

"Yes, Sir! I sure am."

"Well, this Army needs a French linguist to work the Cambodian problem. We've been putting in a personnel request to Headquarters for a French linguist every month for the past eight months. We're short two."

"But, Sarge," I tried to explain. "I am a trained Vietnamese linguist fresh out of school. I'm primed and ready to go to work using my training."

"I'm going to run it by the Old Man this evening, Fournier. But I am damn sure that you can count on working the Cambodian problem using your French language skills. See me in the morning at 0715. Now get the hell out of here before I change my mind."

I was stunned. I had just spent one year at Ft. Meade studying one of the more difficult Asian languages, busting my ass in the language lab, staying up all night cramming for tests, and now they were going to put me to work as a goddamn French linguist! I was pissed—really pissed! At this precise moment I felt a hand on my shoulder.

"Hey, *mon frere*, I'm George Ronson. We'll be working together. The guys just told me that my prayers for help have been answered."

He stuck out his hand to shake mine. I noticed that Ronson was an SP5, was smoking a smelly Gitane French cigarette, and was wearing tinted glasses with European-style frames.

He smiled and said, "Come on. let's go over to the NCO Club and I'll let you know what's going on."

We sat down at a corner table and Ronson motioned to the bartender to send over two bottles of Export 33, a French beer referred to as "bawmy ba." When the beers arrived, Ronson handed me a Gitane, lit it, and proposed a toast.

"To our new frog. May his legs never fail him!"

I laughed out loud and clinked my bottle with his. I liked this guy. He seemed mellow and continental.

"Where did you learn to croak," I asked.

"My father was in the US Army stationed in France after the Second World War. I attended French schools for eight years."

He was obviously educated and I liked that! I leaned closer to him and asked the question that was first and foremost on my mind,

"OK, what's this Cambodian problem that Pribble's going to assign me to?"

Ronson thought for a second, then leaned over and began to whisper in my face.

"We've got four Frenchies working the problem, two during the day and two in the evening. You and I will be working the evening shift. We got 058s (Morse Intercept Operators) churning out *beaucoup* pages of Cambodian military communications. We do the decrypts and the translations. Cushiest duty in this unit."

"How's that?" I inquired.

I knew there had to be a catch somewhere. This entire proposition seemed entirely too easy. Ronson's face lit up like a street light at dusk.

"You know those guys you just checked in with? Well, they're all going out into the field to work alongside the infantry. Some of them will be carrying 65-pound radios on their backs while slogging through snake and leech-infested paddies and canals. And where will you and I be? Sitting in an air-conditioned building in our swivel executive chairs, smoking Gitanes, and generally fucking off. You know, trying to make thirty minutes work last seven hours. Do you play chess?"

"No. But I really like bridge."

Ronson let out a hearty laugh at my reply.

"We'll have to wait and hope that we get two more Frogs so that we have a foursome." I tried to get serious for a moment but this was one large bite to chew.

"Who do we report to?" I asked.

This was just too unbelievable.

"Major Beauville. We'll see him once or twice a month," Ronson replied with a smile.

"You're shitting me. Once or twice a month?"

I had to stop and take a deep breath. My face broadcast total disbelief and I slapped my cheeks to confirm that I was not just dreaming this whole thing. I stood and took a final slug of beer.

"See you tomorrow," I shouted as I headed out the door.

I walked back toward my assigned barracks and could only shake my head in wonder at the mysterious ways in which the US Army operates.

Chapter 9
May 1966

Mano a Mano

The 175th RRC Company was located on the perimeter of Saigon's main airport, Tan Son Nhut. It was through this airport that eighty percent of our troops filtered in and out of Vietnam. As soon as the men of the 175th touched down in the area, they had to learn to eat, sleep, and drink to the constant roar of jet planes; they had to learn to shut out the incessant whirr of Huey helicopters that swarmed around the area like restless bees looking for an empty hive.

The entire perimeter of our company area was surrounded by an 8-foot chain link fence topped with barbed wire and located about 10 feet beyond the bunker that encircled us. This bunker, covered by large metal panels on top of which were stacked three layers of sandbags about 3 feet deep and 3 feet wide, provided the layers of fortification around our compound. Rough-hewn entrances were gouged out of the earth at 25-foot intervals around the trench.

One work building was located approximately 500 yards from the company area in a section that housed five large hangars and several aircraft maintenance shops. My first assignment was in this building. Exactly as promised, I was assigned to the 4:00 P.M. to midnight shift and every afternoon six of us wolfed down an early dinner and headed out to work by 3:45. To exit the company area we were required to walk between the sandbags to the north and pass through an open gate in the fence. About 50 yards outside the perimeter, we crossed a bridge over a small river.

This small waterway became significantly important to us because five kilometers upriver was the home of the 161st US Army Mortuary Detachment. Here bodies were embalmed, prepared for funeral services, and put in aluminum caskets for shipment home. During the embalming process, blood was routinely dumped into the river. The six of us could always tell how intense the fighting was throughout the country by the color of the water and the acrid odors emanating from it. The deeper the color red, the heavier the fighting. We always felt relieved when the river water was clear or a very light pink.

After crossing the river, we headed along the tarmac toward the first hangar where we could see a Lockheed C5A Galaxy with its rear door open in an aircraft parking area. Every day forklifts removed large containers of equipment coming into the country and refilled the aircraft with the aluminum caskets destined for delivery to the west coast of the US. The caskets were stacked six high, five across, and twenty deep in groups of ten to fifteen. The smell of propane exhaust from the forklift motors hung heavily in the air so we never lingered long.

As we walked toward our work building we passed numerous fighter jets parked in neat rows along the airstrip. Busy airmen reloaded the wing pods with rockets and other ordinance. Periodically an air policeman would wave as he made his evening rounds with his German Shepherd sentry dog. I would then head for my desk and settle in to the nightly routine of decrypting and translating Cambodian military communications conducted in French.

At the end of our shift the six of us would meet outside the front entrance of our building and retrace our steps back to the company area. If we were hungry, we headed to the NCO club for a hamburger and beer. Because of my day job teaching English at *The British School*, most often I headed straight for bed.

Such was the case on the night of October 21, 1966, when I was abruptly forced to modify this mundane routine.

My cubicle, located next to the back door at the very end of the row provided easy access for a quick dash into bed. I had returned and I was perched on the edge of my cot one boot short of total collapse when ALL HELL BROKE LOOSE! I raced to the back door and peered out. Abruptly, a large blast nearly knocked me to the floor! And then another! I fell backward and bounced off my wooden wall locker.

"Holy shit," I yelled. "Those are mortar rounds!"

Quickly the other men in the barracks grabbed their steel pots and M-16s, and headed for the bunkers. I did the same. Here I was in a narrow bunker ready for war—wearing only a steel pot, one boot, and a pair of O.D. boxer shorts.

At this moment I had my first insightful realization: *none of us had any ammunition.*

In the distance I heard someone shout, "Get some ammo down here!"

BAROOM!! Another mortar round fell very near to our position. The concussion slammed me to the ground.

I could hear someone frantically yelling, "Where's the armorer."

And then came the staggering response: "Rhyman's downtown and he's the only one with a key to the ammo locker."

"You're shitting me!" I bellowed.

Why did everything get crazier and crazier in this crazy war?

"You heard me, Rhyman's downtown."

Obviously, no one could believe the impossible quagmire in which we suddenly found ourselves.

"Quick, someone find Lawler!" the guy next to me yelled.

The company supply sergeant would surely have a way out of this. But I had my doubts. I broke out in a cold sweat as a paralyzing fear settled in on me.

"He's downtown, too," came the response.

We looked at one another in desperation. Here we were, face-to-face with death, and neither an officer to direct us nor a bullet to defend ourselves.

"Hey, we found some tracer rounds," someone yelled. "Everyone take four."

Terror does strange things. I felt something warm and wet run down the back of my legs. I reached down and brought my fingers up to my nose. Son-of-a-bitch, I had just shit my pants!

I grabbed four tracer rounds and somehow managed to chamber one. I pointed my weapon through the 6" x 9" firing window and waited. In the distance I could hear North Vietnamese voices shouting incoherently to their troops in front of me.

Oh my God, they're North Vietnamese out there. I aimed into the darkness and pulled the trigger. One tracer round exploded and lit up the area about 50 yards in front of me.

Oh, God! The voices were getting closer. Another mortar round landed nearby. I could hear numerous other explosions sounding in the distance and was momentarily stunned. I chambered and fired another tracer round in the general direction of the voices. Suddenly, the guy to my right panicked.

He dashed out of the bunker and headed toward the center of the company area screaming, "I'm hit! I'm hit! I'm hit!"

Those of us who remained in the bunker might just as well have been shooting blanks. Tracer rounds, designed to light up an area so that live bullets can be fired more accurately, can at best hope to inflict first-degree burns at 50 yards, but not much else. Without officers or senior enlisted men to lead us, we were on our own and chasing windmills. I felt sure that I was dead meat.

All of a sudden a loud command cut the confusion. From the depths of a bunker some 75 yards away, 2nd Lieutenant Graham was calling the shots.

Orders were being passed down the line from soldier to soldier until the message finally reached our area:

"Unsheathe bayonets and prepare for hand-to-hand combat."

When I realized what had been ordered, my bowels rebelled again!

Never had I been so totally traumatized. Nothing in my past had even remotely prepared me for the terror that now burned in my gut. Parents. Wife. Home. Jersey hills. No thought could calm the terror that raged within me.

To my left another soldier panicked. As he unsheathed his bayonet, he managed to gash the palm of his left hand. Screaming in pain, he waved his M-16 in the air, managing to jab the point of his bayonet into a gap in the metal panel that served as the bunker ceiling. At the same time he punctured several sandbags that slowly began to drizzle sand on top of us. So here we were, tracer rounds in hand, being buried alive little by little.

But was I worried? No way! I was prepared because I had had *ONE* glorious hour of bayonet training during basic training at Ft. Dix! We had all dutifully queued up waiting our turn to attack a straw mannequin by ramming our bayonet into its immobile midsection. We screamed good old American curse words and demeaning epithets, lunged ruthlessly, then got in line to do it all over again!

Just when things were looking their bleakest, the Air Force showed up. And not only did they show up, they miraculously showed up with a "Jolly Green Giant" (JGG). The JGG was an old DC-3 outfitted with Gatling guns in the doorways on both sides of the aircraft. This plane was capable of saturating a large area below with hot lead. Some airman later told me that the Gatling guns could put down one round per square foot per second. In any case, this DC-3 could fly at a relatively slow speed over a targeted area and wipe out anything that moved. I just squatted where I was and listened.

The roar was deafening. I could hear men screaming as they were literally cut in half by a hail of bullets. And then suddenly everything became ominously quiet. Soon, I heard the Lieutenant ordering us to get out of the bunker and return to our barracks. It was about 2:15 A.M. I was exhausted, both mentally and physically. Without bothering to take off my boxer shorts or boot, I walked slowly to the showers and let the water wash over me.

At the crack of dawn, the entire company was assembled for roll call. Only one of our men was missing—his mangled body found later in the morning, a victim of suicide. It did not take long to learn that the airbase had come under attack by North Vietnamese regulars whose mission had been to blow up as many aircraft as they could using satchel charges. Immediately we were split up into squads and sent out to assess the damage.

My squad headed out the back gate. There were bodies everywhere. As we walked along the tarmac, I saw the bodies of at least ten air policemen with their dead German shepherds. I personally counted eighty-two dead North Vietnamese soldiers, most of them casualties of the Jolly Green Giant. Other severely wounded enemy soldiers were lying in pools of blood, gasping and moaning while several air force doctors and medics performed triage on the most seriously wounded. We also came across twelve handcuffed and blindfolded prisoners who were being guarded by an air force Tech Sergeant, E-6. But we had seen enough of war. We walked right by, turned on our heels, and headed back toward the company area.

Chapter 10
May 1966

Fowl Play

Our Operations Building, also known as White Birch, hummed with around-the-clock activity, as the Morse code intercept operators, cryptanalysts, linguists (translators), communications traffic analysts, and order-of-battle specialists tried to keep up with the high volume of enemy radio communications traffic. Three times daily like clockwork, mess trucks arrived at the Operations Building loaded with hot meals for delivery to hungry soldiers ever eager to take a break and "chow down." The mess hall personnel would wait around to take back any refuse and scraps for disposal by burning.

The underbrush around the Operations Building teemed with small animals and aggressive birds competing for handouts. Generally the cooks took great pride in looking out for these critters and readily doled out handfuls of scraps to their insistent visitors. Most prominent among the noisiest beggars was a pair of vocal peacocks. Daily they strutted their stuff around the yard shrieking for handouts and staging public performances by fanning their tails in a display of variegated plumage and stunning poses. Though the peacocks were raucous and ill-mannered, the cooks obviously favored these exotic birds. The choicest morsels were put aside for them, despite the fact that they would hiss and lunge with open beaks at anyone who ventured too near. Soon after my arrival, I was informed in no uncertain terms that this pair of peacocks ruled the roost and had been residents of the grounds long before the Operations Building was constructed.

When I landed in Vietnam in May 1966, I was a Specialist 5th Class (SP5) Vietnamese linguist. The Commanding Officer of the 175th Radio Research Company and his enlisted administrative aides had previously established a schedule for guarding the Operations Building and other key facilities. The plan was that any new arrival whose rank was E-4 or below would perform one month of guard duty followed by a guaranteed eleven months free of that responsibility. E-5s would fill in only if there was a shortage of grade E-4s and below. The grueling one-month cycle was 8 hours on duty, 8 hours off duty, 8 hours on duty, 8 hours off duty, 8 hours on duty, 24 hours off duty, then start over again. As luck would have it, there was a shortage of lower ranking personnel at the time of my arrival. Thus, I, SP5 Pete Fournier, was assigned this dreaded guard duty. One week into this routine left me drained, quite irritable, and thoroughly homesick. After two weeks my morale had hit rock bottom with a thud!

I awakened one morning to dense fog and a steady drizzle. My specific assignment, to guard the Operations Building from 3:00 P.M. to 11:00 P.M., only underscored my misery as waves of discontent descended with the falling rain. The rain continued during my entire watch, and I was soaked to the bone despite my protective poncho. My soggy boots squeaked with every step and emphasized how dog tired and unhappy I was to be slogging through the mud and rain. Pangs of homesickness gnawed at my gut. And then it happened! I spotted a smooth round rock on the ground. Not too big. Just about the size of a major league baseball. I picked it up and palmed it until it felt just right in my hand. I stopped, rested my M-16 against the building, and gripped the rock just as I had learned in Little League. About 50 feet away in the evening mist I could see the two peacocks. They morphed into Yogi Berra before my very eyes and they seemed to be squatting behind home plate. It was the seventh game of the World Series, bases loaded, last of the ninth inning, 3–2 Yankees, Duke Snider of the Brooklyn Dodgers at the plate. Ebbets Field was going wild! I was Whitey Ford standing on the mound. I squinted in for a sign from Yogi. And then I got it—fastball. I wound up and threw with all my might. The "ball" flew through the air and then bounced two times in the dirt. On the third bounce, it ricocheted off the back of one of the peacocks. The startled bird let out a booming shriek and fluttered away. Thinking nothing more of the incident, I picked up my M-16 and continued to walk around the building. Once again, as I rounded to my "field of dreams," I spotted another perfect rock. Again, the crowd went insane! I got the sign from Yogi and threw another fastball. This time the rock bounced once and hit the other peacock squarely on its side. Again, the crowd roared—or did I hear a shrill screech and the flutter of ruffled feathers? I slung my weapon over my shoulder and continued my rounds.

Minutes later, as I once more turned the corner near the scene of my fantasies, I sensed a large object careening toward me. I ducked and I threw up my hands in self-defense but it was too late. TWO KAMIKAZE PEACOCKS slammed full force into my upper body!

The angry peacocks were doing the Chattanooga Choo Choo on my face. I struggled in vain to get them away, waving frantically and screaming at the top of my lungs. Finally the peacocks fell to the ground, got up, and high-tailed it into the mist. My face was on fire. I looked down but couldn't see a thing. Desperately I tried to wipe the blood from my eyes with my poncho. My uniform front was soaked and blood was splattered everywhere. I was sure I was going to die at any moment. Goddam birds!

In what seemed like an eternity, I managed to stagger over to the entrance to the Operations Building. Too traumatized to talk, I stumbled up to the entry guard, who almost fainted when he saw me.

"My God, Motha'! What the fuck happened to you?"

He looked down in disbelief at the bloody mass that slumped in front of him. Picking up his field phone, he called the Sergeant-of-the-Guard.

"Someone's been shot, Sarge. Send an ambulance. Quick!"

Word spread throughout the building like oil on a hot griddle, sending soldiers scurrying for wet paper towels, toilet paper—anything that would staunch the flow of blood.

By the time the ambulance jeep arrived I had composed myself and wiped the blood from my face. I jumped into the back seat and the driver took off at high speed toward the Navy medical facility about 3 kilometers away. We screeched to a halt in front of the building around 10:00 P.M., and since I was ambulatory, the driver waited outside while I walked in. Straight ahead was a counter behind which a medical corpsman slept soundly in his chair. One tap on the counter jolted him into action. When he opened his eyes, I'm sure he believed that someone from "The Land of the Living Dead" had just walked in.

He stood, looked me up and down, and exclaimed, "Jesus Christ! What truck hit you?"

I sucked in my breath, tried to look alive, and gave him the only response that I could think of.

"I was attacked by two peacocks," I answered lamely.

"Yeah, tell me another one, GI."

This corpsman obviously was used to plenty of bullshit from cocky soldiers who passed though sick bay.

"You've got to come up with something better that that!"

"No, I'm serious. I was on guard duty and I *was* attacked by two peacocks."

The improbability of my story overwhelmed us both for he was not about to fall for a preposterous tale couched in such obvious fantasy; and I was not about to give in to the futility of trying to explain my ridiculous situation.

"You're the biggest lyin' piece of shit I've ever seen. You've been in a bar fight, right?"

Still incredulous, he eyed me with obvious disdain and disbelief. All I could do was stand there dumbly in my guard duty uniform while droplets of blood dripped down my face and onto the floor. I took a deep breath and tried to explain again.

"Wrong again, swabbie," I insisted. "Goddamit, I *was* attacked by peacocks."

By now my face was burning up and the pain had started to settle in big time!

"Stay right where you are, soldier! I want the Lieutenant to see this one."

The stunned and unbelieving corpsman turned and disappeared through a door at the back of the room. Indignant and dazed, I stood immobilized at the counter, totally frustrated and humiliated, a painful blob of humanity completely caked in blood.

The door flew open and in barged a Navy Lieutenant with the corpsman right on his heels. As he got closer I could make out through my blood-shot eyes that his nametag read "Dr. Lewis." Lewis came around the counter and stood with his nose six inches from the tip of mine.

"Alright soldier, where was the bar brawl?"

He was gruff, impatient, and obviously not in the mood to take any guff from the likes of me.

"Honest sir, I was attacked by peacocks!" I muttered.

His mocking laughter sent waves of frustration and fear up and down my spine, making me wonder if my story would ever be believed.

"OK then, let's have a closer look," he barked.

The corpsman produced a washbasin with warm soapy water. I removed my shirt, undershirt, and pants. As the caked blood was washed away it became obvious to both the doctor and the corpsman that my face had several hundred hairline scratches. The profuse bleeding had masked this fact.

Finally the doctor relented.

"OK, you win."

He turned directly to the corpsman and shouted directions.

"Corpsman, prepare a tetanus shot, bring me alcohol wipes and an astringent pack. Let's get this ridiculous avian disaster taken care of!"

After an hour of medical cleanup, I was returned to duty. The jeep driver took me back to the company area. I threw my shirt and pants into a trash bin and put on a new uniform for a fresh start. When I returned to my duty station, those obnoxious "kamikaze peacocks" were still strutting back and forth as if they owned the place, only rekindling my already "fowl" mood.

Fortunately, I was never again assigned guard duty at the Operations Building, for I possibly would have been tempted to go after the two culprits with my loaded M-16. "Kamikaze" court martial avoided! I could only hope that, maybe someday, justice "would be served" at some Vietnamese family dinner!

Chapter 11
May–June 1966

Lightning Strikes

The week after my run-in with the peacocks I was griping about enlisted life to one of my buddies in the barracks. After several long minutes of complaints, SP5 Sanchez was fed up with my bitching.

Fournier," he commented, "if you're so damned unhappy with things as they are, why don't you become an officer and suffer in style? You'd maybe gain some respect and certainly make out better 'pay wise.'"

I laughed out loud and spat some sarcastic and uncomplimentary remarks about officers in general.

"Furthermore," Sanchez continued, "I'd be willing to wager $100 that you could not get a direct commission in the U.S. Army."

His contention was that I was not officer material and he was willing to put his money where his mouth was. Indignant, I impulsively put out my hand to seal the wager. Several other enlisted men joined the conversation, witnessed the bet, and laughed hilariously at my bravado. I stomped out of the barracks and headed straight for the Company administrative offices where I barged into the orderly room.

"What do I need to do to apply for a direct commission?" I demanded of the Company clerk.

The clerk broke out laughing at my foolhardy request, but immediately contained himself.

"You need to fill out the appropriate forms, be interviewed and recommended by the Old Man, be further interviewed and recommended by the Battalion Commander, pass a physical, get your Senator back home to introduce a bill in your behalf, and kiss every butt that you can get near," he responded.

"Can you get me the forms?" I inquired.

At this point I was steaming mad and ready to storm the Bastille to get what I was asking.

"You're not serious are you?" he retorted.

Angry as I was, I had to acknowledge that my request was certainly not something that any ordinary soldier in this man's army would have expected. The clerk hardly could be faulted for his sense of disbelief.

Suddenly a door opened and the Company Commander, Captain Whitman, emerged from his office. He had overheard the entire discussion and wanted to add his two-cent's worth.

"Get Fournier the forms, and do it today," he ordered.

Then turning to me he announced, "I think that you would make a fine officer. After all, you survived a vicious attack from two very irate peacocks!"

Although I was not completely sure where he was coming from, I managed a weak smile. Was he being sarcastic? Was he serious?

Not one to question my luck, I replied, "Thank you sir," and turned to leave as quickly as my size 9Ds could carry me.

The next day the Company clerk delivered a packet of forms while I was eating lunch in the NCO Club. He advised me that he needed them back by the next morning, so I took them over to a table and began to neatly fill out each page. A good four hours later the project was complete. I was bound and determined to prove to those jokers back in the barracks that I could be a good officer.

The next morning I returned the forms to the Company clerk. He told me that the CO wanted to see me ASAP. I knocked on his door and was told to come in. I saluted and he motioned for me to sit down. Captain Whitman took some paperwork out of his desk and informed me that he could do an immediate on-site interview to accompany the application that was going up to Battalion.

Surprised but willing, I agreed and Whitman proceeded to fire a long catalogue of standardized questions at me.

"Why do you want to be an officer? What do you think you can contribute? How would you handle the following situations? Do you have the knowledge and military experiences necessary to be an officer?"

I came up with every logical answer I could think of, and interspersed each response with complimentary statements about the Captain's management style, the advantages of Army life, the excellent organization of the 175th RRC, and anything else that came to mind. He seemed impressed! After about thirty minutes, he had taken enough notes to satisfy him that I was a good officer candidate. He assured me that he would send a strong personal recommendation along with the interview transcript. I was flabbergasted. I really didn't want to be part of the officer corps, but circumstances were beginning to move me inexorably in that direction. Changing my mind now would make me the laughing stock of the entire unit.

Two days later, the Company clerk notified me that a Colonel Brewster from Battalion was coming for a visit and wanted to interview me the next day. He handed me a physical exam form, and told me to take care of it within forty-eight hours. That same afternoon the Supply Sergeant found me in the barracks and delivered a message that the CO wanted to discuss my Physical Training test.

I jokingly asked if I could practice for a few days, but his terse response, "Get over to my office and pick up your results," caught me off guard.

"Huh, what are you talking about?" I asked.

I knew that I had not taken any PT test to date and was confused by his firm directive.

Sensing my surprise, the Sergeant winked and said, "Oh, didn't you know that you passed the PT test this morning? The CO told me that you were in excellent shape, and conducting the test would be a waste of everyone's time."

I couldn't believe my ears. Everything was happening so quickly! Was it that the Army wanted me sent out into the field as a forward artillery observer? The rumor was that their average lifespan was four hours!

As scheduled, Colonel Brewster came to visit the 175th RRC the following morning and, after he had conducted his business with Captain Whitman, asked to see me.

"Fournier, you are to be commended for your dedication and for your desire to serve your country in a higher capacity."

I stood at attention beside Whitman's desk while the Colonel continued. "I've just one more question and this is an important one, so think before you answer: You are marching a column of troops and you notice that the lead soldier is exactly two steps from the edge of a 500-foot precipice. Using only accepted military commands (e.g., halt, to the rear march, about face, etc.) how would you stop the column without any loss of life?"

Mentally I gagged.

"How the fuck should I know?" I asked myself.

But mentally I began to run through all of the commands that I had learned in basic training. I could yell "Halt!"— but then it dawned on me that the "Halt!" command would entail three steps: one for the command, then two to stop. The lead man would go over the precipice. For the life of me I couldn't think of an answer. And then, as if I were divinely inspired, it came to me. A smile crept across my face.

"Sir, I would yell 'GAS! That would allow the troops to break the formation, disperse, and hit the ground immediately."

"Brilliant! Absolutely brilliant, Fournier! You are the first soldier to answer that question correctly in my twenty-two years in the Army."

I could tell that I had made a huge impression and could only thank some lucky star for providing my quick inspiration. In a split second I had vaguely remembered discussing the issue of marching and a CBR (Chemical, Biological, and Radiological) attack with my drill sergeant in basic training. My subconscious had come to my rescue!

Minutes that seemed like hours finally passed until, amid congratulations and commendations, I was dismissed. I saluted smartly and left the office armed with the Colonel's endorsement and a promise of his strong recommendation to accompany my application. As I walked back to the barracks, my head was spinning. Some unseen force was at work! Why was my application being expedited like this? I had no ready answer.

I sat down and wrote a letter to my parents about the chain of events. I asked my father, who was active in political circles in New Jersey, if he could use his contacts with the offices of New Jersey senators Clifford Case and Harrison Williams to ask if one of them would sponsor a rider to a Senate bill confirming my commission as a 2nd Lt. in the U.S. Army.

About three weeks later I received a letter from home. Senator Clifford Case had agreed to sponsor a bill in Congress on my behalf. Was this really happening to me? A week later the Company clerk delivered a message that Captain Whitman wanted to see me "immediately, if not sooner." He smiled, letting me know that he couldn't tell me a thing about anything. And deep down I was beginning to hope that the whole thing had fallen through.

Whitman met me at the door of his office and placed a fatherly hand on my shoulder. Once inside, he turned to me and saluted.

"Congratulations, Lieutenant Fournier. We're going to have a little ceremony for you this afternoon up at Battalion. So, report here at 1300 hours."

I was shell-shocked, and truly didn't know what to say. I saluted numbly, turned, and walked out of the office.

At 1300 hours. I reported back to the Captain starched, spit-shined, and "squared away." Then three of us, the Captain, a driver from the motor pool, and I, took off for Battalion headquarters in Long Bien. Thirty minutes later we arrived, parked the jeep, and were greeted by Colonel Brewster who led us into the Officers' Dining Room. One of the 1st Lieutenants moved some tables around to make an open area where we could all stand comfortably. Feeling foolish and somewhat apprehensive, I stood at attention while Brewster swore me in and pinned the camouflaged bars on my uniform. I was now an officer and a gentleman by act of Congress! Suddenly I realized that I was wearing 2nd Lieutenant bars with Specialist 5th Class stripes on my uniform. I removed my shirt and took my penknife out of my pocket. I carefully cut the threads that fastened the SP5 patches and removed each of them. The dark green outline where they were sewn stood out as if in defiance of their removal. I felt as if kindergarten "show and tell" had come to Battalion headquarters as we stood and laughed at the forlorn shirt, now stripped of its rank, which had once been my dress uniform. Colonel Brewster "ordered" me to buy new uniform shirts and start wearing them within twenty-four hours.

I suggested to Captain Whitman that we return to Saigon right away so that I could get this taken care of, but he told me that Brewster and the Lieutenants wanted to have a couple of celebratory drinks at the Officers Club. I looked him in the eye and, with a straight face, told him that I was a Mormon. Whitman took my bait, hook, line, and sinker (even though my dog tags identified me as an Orthodox Druid).

On the way back to Saigon, Whitman announced that he wanted me moved out of the enlisted barracks and into the BOQ (Bachelor Officer's Quarters) by 2200 hours. He also informed me that he really did not have a slot for a 2nd Lieutenant in the Company management hierarchy, but that he would create a new position for me. I would become the first officer in the 175th RRC to hold the title of "Laundry and Morale Officer." Tongue in cheek, I asked him precisely what the job entailed.

His reply was a classic: "You will be responsible to make sure that all laundry comes back from the Vietnamese laundry on a timely basis and in good condition. Additionally, you are to monitor morale in the unit and report back to me on a monthly basis."

All I could do was shake my head in wonderment. I was absolutely flabbergasted that the entire application process and approval had taken only three weeks. So much had happened in such a short time that my mind had not yet sorted out this strange chain of events. And, oddly enough, this was only the beginning. . .

On the morning of my second day on the job as "L & M" (Laundry & Morale) Officer, two enlisted men came to me for assistance. They explained that there was a serious problem in several of the barracks. I listened intently to their story and decided that this situation called for immediate attention and a prominent notice on the Company bulletin board. I had the Company clerk type up a message that read:

ATTENTION ALL 175TH RRC PERSONNEL

It has been brought to my attention that there is an E.M.B.A.T. operating within the Company area. This E.M.B.A.T. is causing many of you to

be very angry and to seek revenge on the perpetrator. We will not tolerate such an individual.
If anyone has any knowledge of who the
E.M.B.A.T. might be, report him immediately to
me or Captain Whitman. A reward of a one-day
pass is being offered for any information leading to the capture and conviction of this
E.M.B.A.T.

2nd Lieutenant Pete Fournier, L & M Officer

Two days went by before anyone questioned me about the contents of the notice.

Then one afternoon the Company clerk took me aside and asked flat out, "Sir, what in the hell is an E.M.B.A.T.?"

Though somewhat embarrassed that he didn't already know, his curiosity had finally gotten the better of him.

I feigned surprise at his ignorance.

Slowly I stood, looked him squarely in the eye, and barked, "Isn't it your job, Corporal, to know all the common acronyms?"

Here I was, still wet behind the ears, lording it over the one soldier who had had the courage to approach me. Why was it that suddenly I was getting a charge out of my newfound power?

"Wait a minute, sir," he replied. "There's no way I can know all 5,000 acronyms in this Goddam Army."

Obviously the clerk was beginning to squirm, and I was beginning to feel a twinge of guilt at my enjoyment of his discomfort.

I looked at him and ginned, "Well, soldier, if you remember only one acronym, remember this one: an E.M.B.A.T is an Enlisted Men's Billeting Area Thief."

He rolled his eyes in disbelief. "That's a new one on me!" he said.

I laughed and replied, "No, it's a new one on me!"

Little did he know that I was the one who had coined the acronym!

The meaning of the E.M.B.A.T. spread quickly throughout the unit. Everywhere I went men were coming up to me and commenting about this wonderful new word. Although over $500 had been stolen, it seemed that attention had been diverted from the seriousness of the problem.

Soldiers began pointing fingers at each other and asking, "Are you the E.M.B.A.T.? I bet you are!"

I received "reliable" information from about fifty individuals that they had identified about twenty different soldiers as the infamous perpetrator. Even the Army C.I.D. (Criminal Investigation Division) sent two investigators to look into the thefts. Two weeks elapsed with no success in finding the E.M.B.A.T.

And then, one morning when I reported to work in the orderly room, SP4 Wilhelm was waiting to see me. He asked if he could speak to me privately. I nodded and led him into the Captain's office and closed the door.

Wilhelm immediately broke down in tears and told me that he was the thief.

He actually said, "Sir, I am the E.M.B.A.T."

I bit my lip and tried to look solemn. He looked so pitiful standing there in front of me.

"My brother just got laid off from his job, and Mom is real short of grocery money," he told me.

I put my hand on his shoulder and sternly admonished him by telling him that there was no excuse for his actions. I told him that he should have come to me when he had the problem and we could have worked something out through Army or Red Cross channels. Wilhelm reached into his pocket and pulled out a small packet wrapped in Kleenex. He unfolded it and a roll of MPCs (Military Payment Certificates) appeared. He counted out exactly $500 onto the desk. I took the money and put it into one of my shirt pockets. Wilhelm began to sob and ask for my forgiveness. I informed him that I understood his circumstances, but that some kind of administrative punishment would have to be meted out. I told him to return to duty and I would get back to him in a day or two. He nodded, saluted, and left the room.

When Captain Whitman came in that morning, I talked the situation over with him. He told me that I should write Wilhelm up and report the incident to Battalion. I asked if we could keep the incident contained within the 175th RRC and take care of it ourselves. He agreed and told me to "handle it." First, I returned the money to its rightful owners. The men wanted to know who the thief was but I told them it was being handled and they should not worry about it. Second, I decided that Wilhelm should be restricted to the Company area for thirty days and perform two extra hours per day of filling sandbags.

Unfortunately, several of the men put two and two together and figured out that SP4 Wilhelm was not doing extra sandbag duty out of the goodness of his heart. They confronted Wilhelm and he broke down and admitted to being the E.M.B.A.T. A few nights later, Wilhelm was dragged from his bunk and beaten pretty badly by "unknown" assailants. Several weeks later I arranged for SP4 Wilhelm to be transferred to another ASA unit up-country in Phu Bai.

Chapter 12
June 1966

Not Every Man's Dream

I had been in Vietnam barely a month when a soldier approached me with an extraordinary proposition. He was rotating back to the States in two weeks and he wanted me to meet someone. SP5 Kendall had been working the 4 P.M. to midnight shift as a Vietnamese linguist and during the day he had a part time job teaching English at a privately owned high school in Saigon, called *The British School*. Currently he was in the middle of a session. Would I, he wondered, be interested in taking his place for the remainder of the term? "The money is good, Pete, and the lady who runs the school is a 'knockout'." *An interesting way to fill my spare time,* I thought.

And so, Kendall and I went downtown to visit *The British School*. He introduced me to Thérèse Bui Thanh, owner and schoolmistress, and recommended me as his replacement. She suggested that I return the next day for an interview.

The following day I arrived at the school by 7:30 A.M. Thérèse was waiting for me in her office and for the next two hours she questioned me about my background and education. During our conversation I exaggerated my qualifications, telling her that I had a bachelor's degree and extensive experience in teaching at the high school level. I had a lot of trouble concentrating, as I was mesmerized by a pair of flashing brown eyes, a long sweep of raven hair, and the most lithesome body that I had yet seen in Vietnam. Thirty-year-old Thérèse had me completely "wowed"! *How could I possibly have been this lucky?* I mused.

During the ensuing conversation, Thérèse revealed that her mother was French and her father, Vietnamese. She also told me that she had returned to Vietnam two years previously after having studied in France and England for six years. The *British School* had been a graduation present from "Daddy." He had had a three-story dilapidated French hotel completely renovated and refurbished as a high school and had turned the entire third floor into living quarters for his daughter.

After grilling me thoroughly, Thérèse asked if I were interested in teaching at *The British School*. Without a moment's hesitation, I blurted out my unqualified "Absolutely!" She informed me that I would teach two classes: the Introduction to English that was already in session and an Advanced English class that would start in two weeks. I was then introduced to Thanh, Thérèse's houseboy and chauffeur. Thanh was a tall, good-looking Vietnamese boy of about eighteen years of age. He bowed and smiled broadly when we were introduced.

About one week later, I came to the school with Kendall to be introduced as his replacement. I sat through his three-hour class to see how and what he was teaching. The students were enthusiastic and eager to learn, a fact that I found quite surprising since the group ranged in age from twelve to forty-five. Kendall had told me previously that the US Embassy and the American armed forces had a large number of bilingual jobs available to Vietnamese. He also indicated that there were at least four more schools of this type in Saigon.

The following Monday, armed with Kendall's textbooks and teaching materials, I arrived for my first day at *The British School*. I was painfully nervous, especially when Thérèse came in twice and sat down to observe, but in general everything seemed to go well. I was assured of this at the end of the class when Thérèse met me and told me how impressed she was with my performance.

"You are a natural teacher, Monsieur Fournier," she said as she shook my hand and told me that she looked forward to seeing me the next day.

I literally "glowed" in the bright light of her approval!

As I was leaving the grounds that first day, I noticed three Americans talking inside the main gate of the school. I stopped to say hello and found out that they also taught at the school. Two of the men were Air Force linguists and one was a civilian from USAID (US Agency for International Development). They asked me how I liked my first day and wondered if I agreed that Thérèse was "hot." I said that I really enjoyed my first day and, absolutely, Thérèse was "quite a good looker."

At the beginning of the third week, I began a new class. "Advanced English Conversation" that was scheduled to meet from 3:00 P.M. to 4:00 P.M. Thérèse had put together a lesson plan that used *The New York Times* and the *Saigon Times* (an English language newspaper) as textbooks. When I walked into the classroom I saw ten middle-aged women sitting at the desks. They all wore elegant silk "ao giai" (the traditional Vietnamese pants with floor length tunics). Thérèse came in, gave me a handwritten class roster, and proceeded to introduce me to my new "students" one by one: Madame Ky, a Madame Thieu, and eight other Madams. It then struck me that each of these women was a South Vietnamese general's wife. Not only that, but Madame Ky was the wife of Air Marshal Nguyen Cao Ky, President of South Vietnam! And, Madame Thieu was the wife of Nguyen Van Thieu who would later be the President during the final fall of Vietnam. I was in a room with ten of the most powerful South Vietnamese women; women who defined the social agenda for Saigon. One was more beautiful than the next. They exuded class and charm. I took a deep breath and told the ladies that we should begin the class. They all dutifully sat down in their student desks as I handed each a copy of the front page of the *New York Times* and officially launched my new class. I was more nervous than a cat in a room full of rocking chairs.

At 3:55 P.M. the class mercifully ended and I hurried out into the street to hail a taxi. Back at Davis Station fifteen minutes later, I hurriedly changed into my uniform and caught a ride out to Operations on the unit's shuttle bus. Previously I had gotten permission from my superiors to be late for work as my teaching was considered a "civic affairs" activity.

Since I now had classes from 9:00 A.M. to 12:30 P.M. and again from 3:00 P.M. to 4:00 P.M., it did not make sense for me to race back to the company mess hall for lunch. As in most hot, tropical countries, a "siesta" period was observed during the hottest part of the day. Vietnam was no exception. During the midday most businesses closed for two hours. The only exceptions were restaurants and bars.

Thus, I decided to eat in one of the many restaurants/ bars on Tu Do Street or over the river in nearby Cholon. In this dubious setting, I fast became the darling of the local bar scene. This young, round-eyed American, competent in Vietnamese, charmed the eager bar girls with his Northern dialect and entertaining wit! At the same time, however, I was picking up the local slang and the Southern equivalents of my Northern vocabulary.

As time went on several of the bar girls sought me out to tell me about their problems with siblings, children, friends, and boyfriends. I was a regular Vietnamese Ann Landers and I was proud when I learned that my Vietnamese name was *Ong Phong* (Mr. Wind). Gradually, I also became friendly with many of the influential mamasans who owned the establishments I frequented. I soon learned that women controlled the local economy of Vietnam because most of the able-bodied men were off at war. The mamasans often gave me free food and drink and, occasionally, free sexual favors.

As I mingled more and more with the people, I learned that a local custom was to rank the value of persons, things, and events using powers of 10. For example, "number 1" was the best, "number 10" was bad, "number 100" was worse, and "number one thou'" was the worst. Thus, if someone was "number 10," they were a bad person. If they "talked number 100," they lied or criticized someone unfairly. If an event was 'number one thou,'" it was the worst thing that could possibly happen. Fortunately, as a person I ranked "number 1" and I talked "number 1." One of my favorite bar girls even wrote "Number 1" with a Magic Marker on a small piece of cloth and sewed it to the back of my olive drab military baseball cap.

When I look back on these days now, I think a possible key to my popularity was that I treated each girl with dignity and respect—despite the fact that every one of them was basically a conniving, two-faced, uneducated slut. Many of these women were infected with gonorrhea and/or herpes. But, virtually all of them had their PhDs in how to peddle "Saigon tea" to unsuspecting customers. This scheme that sought to part soldiers from their money was a favorite ploy among the women. In any case, as a result of my new teaching routine, I would hang out until almost 3:00 P.M. and then take a taxi back to *The British School*.

I had been teaching for about seven or eight weeks when, one afternoon, as I was leaving the school compound, Thérèse asked if I could stop by her office. She sat down at her desk and invited me to pull up a chair and give her a progress report.

"Monsieur Fournier . . . may I call you Pete? How are things going? I hear wonderful reports, but I'm interested to learn how *YOU* feel about your progress."

Alluring as ever, she sat surrounded by papers, books, and a blatant sexuality that nearly sent me reeling across the room. I had a clear view of her cleavage and it was obvious from her body language that she wanted me to see what she had to offer.

"Would you like to join me for lunch on the third floor?" Her mysterious overture caught me off guard but I eagerly complied. "I've something special that I think you'll enjoy."

"I would be honored," I stammered.

My mind had gone blank and I was totally at a loss for something more imaginative to say. *Why was my gorgeous employer coming on to me like this?*

"OK! See you in 10 minutes."

She rose from her chair and walked quickly down the hall to the main staircase. I stepped outside her office and stood transfixed. I could hear her footsteps growing fainter and fainter in the distance. I leaned against the wall and caught my breath. I stared at my watch. 12:55 P.M. The school was empty.

At precisely 1:05 I ascended the main staircase and knocked. Thérèse, wrapped in a silk kimono embroidered with luxurious flowers and gold embossed birds, opened the door and invited me in. She ushered me into her dining room, and gestured toward the chair at the head of the table. I didn't know where to look first: at my "knock-'em-dead" employer or the lavish surroundings in which I found myself. Her home was a virtual palace. Walls sheathed in silk paper, terrazzo marble floors, French provincial furnishings with a Louis XIV motif! Spacious quarters fit for royalty overwhelmed me, but not for long. I had just sat down when there was a knock on the front door and Thanh entered with a large tray of Vietnamese "carry-out" food. As if by magic, Thérèse produced some fine china, silverware, two wine glasses, and a bottle of French Cabernet Rouge.

We sat and talked for what seemed like hours. She told me about her years in Europe and about several failed romances. She asked about my background and sought my opinion on many topics. As we laughed and talked and drank each other in, I fell head-over-heels in love. Therefore, when we'd finished eating and Thérèse suggested a tour of her apartment, I was only too happy to prolong our time together. I readily agreed. She showed me the bathroom with its gold fixtures, vanity, and marble tub; we moved to her den with its shelves of Western classics, and later to the master bedroom with its king-size bed and ornate furniture. She opened the drapes in the corner of the room and eagerly pointed out Saigon, Cholon, and the

Saigon River. The view was incredible and I completely lost myself in the romance of the afternoon. I could see smoke in the distance. I was sure that a battle was being waged about 20 kilometers away.

When I finally turned to leave, my jaw dropped to my knees. Thérèse had slipped out of her kimono and was standing naked at the foot of her bed.

"Can I interest you in some dessert?" she asked unabashedly.

The next hour was a blur as we passionately explored every possible meaning and nuance of the word "dessert"!

I started to get dressed when Thérèse decided that she was not yet fully satisfied. So "around the world" we went again, caught in the whirlwind grip of an uncontrollable passion. I finally got dressed again, gave her a passionate goodbye kiss, and began to leave.

My now intimate employer followed me to the door and promised: "We'll have to do this again sometime."

I nodded in agreement and headed down the stairs to my Advanced English class.

This lunchtime routine continued for many weeks. Thérèse's insatiable appetite for sex was wearing me out. I was "under the gun" to perform daily. She never seemed to tire and I was fading fast! During one of our daily sessions I told her, "Enough is enough; we have to limit our noon-time lovemaking to three times per week, with two times being even better." Hurt and rejected, she at last revealed what I had begun to suspect weeks previously. When living in England, she had been under the care of a psychiatrist who had treated her for nymphomania. I thought to myself, *Just what I need in my life, a nympho! Wasn't it every man's dream to be involved with a nymphomaniac? No way!* I told Thérèse that I would help her with her affliction in any way that I could, but only on the condition that she seek further treatment in Saigon. She agreed and then proceeded to "jump me" one more time.

The next day, Thérèse suggested that we go out for lunch at a restaurant three times per week and eat in two days per week. I readily agreed. I felt that Thérèse would probably not risk "attacking me" in a public place! So, the next day, Thanh chauffeured us in Thérèse's British Humber to one of her favorite restaurants. I made sure that we dined leisurely so that we arrived back at *The British School* just in time for my 3 P.M. class.

Chapter 13
July 1966

The Blessing

The Cambodian Armed Forces was one of our primary intercept targets. Since all of their military communications were conducted in French, we had easily broken their encryption schemes and were readily able to translate from French into English. Three French linguists on staff worked strictly on the "Cambodian Problem," and we knew from aerial photos and agents on the ground that the Ho Chi Minh trail ended very near the Vietnam–Cambodian border in an area hotly disputed by the two countries. Locals had also provided hard evidence that the NVA were using Cambodian territory as a staging area for raids into South Vietnam. What was lacking at the time was corroborative electrical and communications intelligence, known respectively as ELINT and COMINT. Our aim was to acquire this intelligence by monitoring Cambodian military communications.

Many of the messages intercepted at this time were signed by individuals named Lt. Colonel Lon Nol, Captain Pol Pot, and Colonel Hun Sen. These three men would later gain international notoriety for their wanton butchery of their own people. In addition, it was not unusual for some of the messages to originate from the office of Prince Norodom Sihanouk, the nominal head-of-state. Thus, we at the 175th RRC had been trying for about a year to find the "smoking gun" intercept that would confirm via ELINT/COMINT that the NVA were using Cambodian territory as a staging and recuperative area. We had all the visual proof that suggested this but, without ELINT/ COMINT confirmation, the facts were always in doubt.

In early July 1966 one of our French linguists was going through the day's intercepts when he spotted some unusual coordinates in one of the messages. A quick look at a map revealed the coordinates to be about 10 kilometers (6 miles) inside Cambodian territory. The message concerned complaints brought to the Provincial Governor by a peasant who resented NVA soldiers rustling his cattle and pigs for food. Of special interest was the fact that the precise location of the peasant's hut was given. This innocent message became extremely important since it was the first hard evidence acquired through non-human means that substantiated our suspicion that the NVA were active within Cambodian territory.

As the Officer-in-Charge that evening, I read and reread the translation, attempting to verify even the smallest detail. Finally I made a judgment call that this particular message was significant enough to pass on to DOD (the Department of Defense) using the code "CRITIC," an extremely high priority code that in some cases might warrant notification of the President at any time of the day or night. In order to send a message with this high priority, however, the signer had to be a field grade officer (Major or above). I looked at my watch—11:00 P.M. local time. Where in the hell would

I find a field grade officer at this hour? I determined that my best bet was to head for the main BOQ (Batchelor Officer's Quarters) in downtown Saigon. I put the translation in my shirt, headed for the unit motor pool, jumped into one of the jeeps, and sped away. Fortunately, the guards at the front gate bought the story that I was on a critical mission and they let me pass without incident.

Within minutes I was parked across the street from the BOQ. I didn't have to wait long. A tall imposing American with a Vietnamese "hog" in tow soon came shuffling down the street and walked toward one of the exterior rooms. The soldier was passionately hugging and kissing his escort while trying to walk a straight line. He fumbled for his key and entered the room while I darted across the street to the door he had closed. The sign posted to the right read *Col. Mumphrey*.

I had found a field grade officer on the first try! Brazenly I knocked, heard some quick scrambling and a muffled exchange, and finally stared into the bloodshot eyes of the Colonel who now peered through a three-inch opening in the door. In the background I could see the disheveled Vietnamese woman cowering on the bed and clutching her bra and panties.

The bleary-eyed Colonel mumbled, "What do you want?"

His drunken breath nearly knocked me over, but I held my ground. The man had the credentials I needed!

"Sir, I need to speak to a field grade officer," I blurted out.

Quick action was crucial here and I was painfully aware that every second wasted meant time gained for the Viet Cong.

"What about?"

Obviously the man had other things on his mind and I wasn't one of them.

"Hurry this up. Can't you see I'm busy?"

He held tightly to the doorjamb, barely able to stand erect and eager to move on to other business at hand.

"We can't talk here," I responded.

The urgency in my voice must have sobered him a bit, for he opened the door enough so I could see that he was wearing only his olive drab boxer shorts and T-shirt.

"Wait a fuckin' minute," he growled and slammed the door.

When the Colonel re-emerged, he had put on his fatigue pants and flip-flops.

"I'll ask you again, Lieutenant. What in hell do you want at this hour?"

"Sir, I have a high priority message that needs to be sent to DOD and I need a field grade officer to sign off on it."

By this time I was so geared up that nothing seemed more important than getting an authorized signature and racing back to camp.

"Where's the message?" he demanded.

"In my shirt, sir."

This conversation was wasting time, though I could see the Colonel's head was beginning to clear and the seriousness of the situation was beginning to filter through.

"In your fucking shirt!" he boomed.

I stood back, suddenly afraid he'd take a swing at me. He was big, burly, and definitely not a man I'd challenge to a fight.

"Yes sir! I think that you need to see it."

"Lemme see it, Lieutenant," he demanded.

He thrust out a large hairy hand, and I could tell from the tone of his voice that my message had hit its mark. I had definitely piqued his interest.

"Sir, you'll have to come back with me to our Operations. You can only see this communication if you are in a secure area."

All the hours and months of training came to the fore and I knew that it was essential that we play this by the book. I had not come this far only to fumble my responsibilities.

"Alright! Alright! Give me a minute."

He went back into his room and I could hear the woman begin to cry and curse. Finally, the two of them came out and the Colonel, now focused and sober, shoved the lady in the general direction from which they had come. She disappeared into the darkness.

"Come on, let's go," he demanded.

We got into the jeep and I started it up. The canvas top and plastic windows were in place because it was the middle of the rainy season. I had turned on the headlights and was just about ready to put the jeep in gear when the Colonel grabbed my elbow.

"Stop," he ordered. "We don't have to move from right here."

"Excuse me, sir?" I responded.

This night was packed with surprises, one heaped piggyback on top of another!

The Colonel sat erect and stared straight ahead through the windshield. In the dim light from the dashboard I could see that he had raised his right hand and had begun to slowly move it horizontally and vertically in a cross-like motion.

Dramatically he intoned: "By the power invested in me by the Congress of the United States, I declare this jeep to be a secure area."

I was struck speechless. I had just witnessed "the blessing of the jeep." Not even the Pope could have done it with more flair! I was now sitting in a secure area. He and I could discuss classified information at will. Anything that we said would never be heard by anyone who didn't have the appropriate security clearance. All it took was a wave of the hand—a hand empowered with the proper authority!

The Colonel took the flashlight that was on the passenger side floor and shined it in my face.

"Let me see what you've got," he ordered.

I unbuttoned my shirt and extracted the highly classified document. He grabbed it out of my hand and began to examine it by the light of the flashlight.

"What does this mean?" he demanded.

I told him in twenty-five words or less the significance of what he was reading. The Colonel reached for the pen in my shirt pocket, signed the document, and leaned out of the jeep. He proceeded to puke his guts out. The stench of booze, beer, and vomit settled over the jeep and I suddenly found myself becoming nauseous.

"Get the fuck out of here," he ordered.

He half fell out of the jeep and began to stagger back across the street. I popped the clutch and sped away.

The next day I showed a copy of the message to the Officer-in-Charge and explained what had transpired. The only bit of "deviation" was that the Colonel had returned to Operations with me and had signed the message inside the building. The OIC commented that the piece of paper he was holding had a foul odor to it. I shrugged and pleaded complete ignorance of the situation. Two days later, the OIC told me that I had done the right thing and commended me on my professionalism. If only the jeep could talk!

Chapter 14
September 1966

The Color Purple

"ASAP Fournier! The Old Man wants to see you—yesterday!"

PFC Williams had just sprinted seventy-five yards to breathlessly inform me that the Company Commander, Captain Whitman, had issued a summons.

"Good God! What have I done now?" I exploded.

Several months had passed since the "Peacock Encounter" and my life seemed to have settled into some semblance of normalcy. But this order did not bode well.

The knowing smile that spread over Williams' face indicated clearly that something weighty was afoot. A quick about face and I was headed for the orderly room.

When I arrived, the clerk ushered me directly into Captain Whitman's office. Breathlessly I saluted, and then automatically shook the hand that the Captain offered.

His eyes danced as he said, "Congratulations, Fournier. Your citation paperwork has been approved by Battalion."

"What are you talking about, Sir?"

I was truly puzzled, though the Captain seemed to think I was well aware of what was going on.

"You know! Your Purple Heart paperwork."

He leaned back in his chair and looked at me with what almost seemed like a sense of perverted fatherly pride.

"What Purple Heart, Sir?"

This conversation was beginning to take on a surreal glow.

"Oh come on, Fournier, you don't need to play dumb with me."

He sat upright and literally seemed to gloat as he eyeballed my discomfort. I did not particularly like or trust this man who apparently took delight in my embarrassment.

"With all due respect, Sir, I really *don't* know what you're talking about."

Suddenly selected pieces of the last month fell into place and I began to suspect that my worst fears were about to be realized.

"OK, Fournier, here's the entire skinny."

By this time he was so pleased with himself and the announcement he was about to make that I wanted to slam my fist into his gut.

"Remember your encounter with those two feral birds?"

"How could I possibly have forgotten it!"

"Well, I have found an Army Regulation under which you qualify for the Purple Heart because you sustained potentially disabling injuries while in a combat zone and while performing your assigned duties."

I stared in disbelief as he continued.

"You see, Fournier, it's a win-win situation. It gives you something to brag about, but it also looks good for me and for the unit to have a Purple Heart under our belts. The more Purple Hearts I have in my Company, the better it looks in my file. Every award increases my chances of making Major."

I stood dumbfounded. I couldn't believe that any sane officer would do this to one of his men.

"Sir, did you write up the recommendation for the award?"

Something in me still hoped against hope that this was a joke; some sick dream from which I would suddenly wake to find the world still turned smoothly on its axis.

"Sure did!"

By this time the good Captain Whitman was playing out the situation—no holds barred.

"Sir, can I go home to the States tonight and we'll call it even?" Whichever way I turned, I saw no easy escape from what I presumed to be an ignominious fate. How could I possibly explain a Purple Heart for being attacked by two *peacocks!*

"Not on your life, Lieutenant. The Battalion is having their monthly awards ceremony and parade next week up in Long Bien. You had better be there or your ass is mine."

"Sir, can't we just call this whole thing off? Aren't you aware that I was teasing those birds when they attacked me?"

"Doesn't matter, Lieutenant Fournier. The incident meets all of the Army's requirements for an award."

No matter what I said to try to convince Captain Whitman to change his mind, I knew I was soon to be subjected to what would most certainly be the height of ignominy. Pushing his chair back from the desk, the Old Man stood, and flatly refused to discuss the matter further. Indeed, he verbally threw me out of his office.

Battalion Headquarters in Long Bien was about 30 kilometers northeast of my base at Tan Son Nhut airport. The Battalion oversaw infantry, armored supplies, artillery, helicopter/fixed wing, human intelligence, maintenance, engineering, administrative facilities, and electronic intelligence units. Each month, an awards ceremony was held to distribute the medals earned by members of the various commands. The formal procedure took place on a small parade field bounded on either side by primitive metal stands set up for visiting VIPs, observers, and guests. The observers were usually Battalion HQ staff members who had been "encouraged" to attend, even if it were their day off or if they had been on duty all night. The medal recipients stood one arm's length apart in a line. A three-person delegation consisting of a senior grade officer (even a general, if one was available), a senior enlisted man, and a junior officer ceremoniously pinned a ribbon with the medal suspended from it to the uniform of each recipient. After an appropriate citation was read, the recipient would again salute the officers and receive their terse verbal congratulations. The three-person party then moved on to the next recipient.

During the week following my meeting with Captain Whitman, word that I was going to be awarded the Purple Heart spread like wildfire. An obvious coolness developed between my fellow soldiers and me, serving to heighten my extreme depression and apprehension. All of us were aware of the heavy casualties being taken by troops in the field and we understood the conditions in which they lived. To be honored for a peacock attack was beyond comprehension! Calls of "Our Hero!" or requests like "Can I touch you, Sir?" followed me wherever I went. I simply wanted to curl up and die because I felt that the whole ordeal was just fucking unfair.

On the appointed day, I was driven to Long Bien by a PFC from the motor pool accompanied by Captain Whitman and the Executive Officer, 1st Lt. Henderson. During the trip I briefly contemplated jumping out of the jeep in hopes of being injured sufficiently to require evacuation to Japan or Clark Airbase for treatment. But, I figured with my luck, I would probably kill myself. I held fast to my seat and we arrived at Long Bien in time for me to be shown to my position in the lineup.

About twenty soldiers waited to be decorated and I had just gotten in place when *The Star Spangled Banner* signaled the opening of the ceremony. The Battalion Commander spoke briefly; but my mind was twelve thousand miles away. Not until the actual pinning ceremony began did I plummet back to earth. My fellow honorees were noteworthy: The first two soldiers in line had been wounded by shrapnel during a mortar attack. The sergeant next to me had been acting as a door gunner on a Huey when the aircraft went down in a barrage of anti-aircraft fire. The helicopter crashed in a dry rice paddy and the sergeant, although gravely wounded, had pulled the pilot and copilot to safety just as the aircraft exploded into flames.

When I realized I was standing beside someone being awarded the Bronze Star with V-device for Valor, I almost fainted dead on the spot! Now the awards party moved directly in front of me.

The junior officer began to read my citation. "ON MAY 5, 1966, SPECIALIST FIFTH CLASS PETER J. FOURNIER, WHILE WALKING HIS POST IN A MILITARY MANNER WAS ACCOSTED BY TWO FERAL PEACOCKS...."

I bit my lip so hard I could taste blood. From the stands behind me I could hear murmurs and muffled laughter. The junior officer paused and glared into the stands. The laughter stopped.

"That's better," said the officer.

Never before in my life had I felt so humiliated! I felt like taking my entrenching tool and digging a hole into which I could disappear.

The awards party moved on. The soldier to my right was also awarded the Bronze Star, but I could hear only echoes of the laughter in the stands behind me. The longest hour in my life ticked on until finally the last award was conferred. I double-timed it back to the jeep without saying a word to anyone. The driver and both officers were already seated and ready to roll. At this moment, I truly believe that Captain Whitman realized what an asshole he had made out of both of us. He never offered congratulations, and not a single word was exchanged during the half hour trip back to the 175th RRC.

When we pulled into the Company area, I jumped out of the jeep and went directly to the Bachelor Officer Quarters. I changed into civilian clothes, put the medal and citation in my pocket, and headed for downtown Saigon. I directed the cab driver to take me to

Cho Lon, the Chinese section of Saigon on the other side of the Saigon River. As we crossed the bridge, the cab driver slowed in the snarled traffic. This was my moment!

I ordered the cab driver to stop, I paid my fare and jumped out. I took the citation from my pocket and tore it into the smallest pieces I could manage. Without ceremony I tossed them over the side of the bridge and watched as they fluttered slowly down to the water. I then took the medal with its fancy ribbon and tried to "Frisbee" it out over the water. Like the leaden feeling in my heart, it plummeted straight down. With a splash it hit the water, floated a few feet, and then gradually sank. I looked around to see half a dozen curious people standing on the bridge watching me.

Totally disconcerted, but relieved that I'd rid myself of an overwhelming burden, I blurted out in Vietnamese the English equivalent of "you'd never understand what this is all about!" and walked briskly back toward Saigon.

I went directly to my favorite bar where I knew all of the girls and the mamasan. She was a good friend and was always a sympathetic ear when I needed to talk. We sat in the back of the bar and she had some Vietnamese food brought in. We ate and drank while I told her the entire "Purple Heart" saga. She seemed to understood completely.

"Mr. Phong, I have never seen you so agitated and depressed. You need to be very happy," she told me in Vietnamese.

"What do you suggest?" I asked.

She motioned to Tuyet, the prettiest girl sitting at the bar and called her over to our table. The mamasan gently stroked Tuyet's arm.

"Mr. Phong needs your love and attention. He is very sad."

Tuyet nodded her understanding and took my hand. She led me through a beaded curtain into one of the back rooms of the bar. An hour later, I left the bar definitely feeling unburdened.

Chapter 15
August 1966

Overheard at Lunch

During the time that Thérèse and I were dating, she told me that she held memberships in two of Saigon's elite clubs: the *Club Nautique* (the "Yacht Club") and the *Circle Sportif* (the "Country Club"). I also learned that she belonged to the Saigon Rotary Club, the Saigon Chamber of Commerce, and that she sat on the Board of Directors of Coca Cola Bottling of Southeast Asia (COKESA). This was quite an impressive résumé for a five-foot-one, ninety-eight pound, thirty-year-old Eurasian bundle of energy. What a catch!

As time went on, I actually considered asking Thérèse to marry me. One major obstacle—I was already married! *Damn!* Boyhood dreams of spending my days as a gigolo on the French Riviera had almost become a reality during this stolen interlude with my Saigon sweetheart.

One day, Thérèse suggested that we have lunch at the *Circle Sportif*. I readily agreed, eager to experience the sights and sounds of Saigon from the privileged perspective of the upper class. Thanh drove us in style in

Thérèse's Humber, winding slowly through crowded streets until we found ourselves parking under the large awning directly in front of the restaurant. We were greeted by a gentleman dressed in a tuxedo who showed us to a table on the terrace, where we could enjoy a view of the river that stretched as far as the eye could see and revealed a busy thoroughfare for passing junks and small fishing craft.

"What a terrific way to get a handle on Saigon," I remarked.

"Tell me about your impressions of Saigon," Thérèse asked with genuine interest.

During the weeks before I had met Thérèse I had spent time walking and riding around Saigon as a "tourist," taking time to purchase several pairs of pants and three shirts that would allow me to blend in with the crowds around me. When I engaged people in conversation, I told them that I was a Canadian working with the United Nations—I truly had a genuine fear of being kidnapped or killed by the Viet Cong!

I had visited the newly completed *Dinh Độc-Lập* or Independence Palace that had been built on the original site of the French governor's headquarters in the late 1800s. I had spent an entire day in the *Bến-Thành* market, a collection of small shops that took up an entire city block and which had been in existence since the French occupation. I must have talked for two hours with the old lady who operated the puppy stall. As we spoke, Vietnamese housewives would stop and pick out a puppy or two, put them in their shopping bags, and continue on their way. It took me several weeks to get over my "culture shock" when I realized that these puppies were not intended as pets. I was also very interested in the open produce markets that sold unusual fruits that only grew in

Southeast Asia. I tried to learn the Vietnamese word for each of these fruits.

I was fascinated by the *Bảo-Tàng Quốc-Gia* or National Museum located in Saigon's Zoo and Botanical garden. The museum housed many historical objects, some dating back to the Han invasion from China, granite tablets with complex carvings, and even the clothing from mandarins and kings from hundreds of years past. Here I saw a statue of Buddha with a thousand arms and a thousand eyes. I spoke with one of the guards who told me that many of the items in the museum date back to the 6th and 7th centuries. I also visited an ancient Chinese pagoda that contained a huge gold Buddha whose ornamentation and coloration overwhelmed my senses. When I told Thérèse of my wanderings she was extremely impressed that I had taken the time.

"Thérèse, darling, your city has been aptly named 'The Pearl of the Orient,'" I remarked. I am jealous that you can live here forever."

"This city is just as romantic as Paris and I love you, Pierre. Maybe *we* can live here together," she purred in French into my ear. "Daddy says that he would like to meet you. I told him all about you. Can you come to dinner one day next week?" I smiled lovingly and squeezed Thérèse's hand.

"I would be honored," I replied.

All at once a small commotion broke out on the terrace to the right side of the main dining room. Busboys suddenly materialized, hurriedly cleared tables and rearranged chairs; waiters scurried busily in all directions and an air of hushed expectation settled over the entire area. Fascinated, we watched as the maitre d' ushered a group of ten men to three tables not far from where Thérèse and I were sitting...and suddenly I realized what all the commotion was about! General William Westmoreland, Ambassador Henry Cabot Lodge, Secretary of Defense Robert McNamara, and Chairman of the Joint Chiefs of Staff, General Harold K. Johnson had come for lunch. With them were six bodyguards for protection.

I immediately switched from English to French and identified the men for Thérèse. She was impressed that such important personages were sitting no more than twenty feet away from our table and her eyes danced with excitement as we continued our conversation in French. How thankful I was that I had made the decision to wear civilian clothes when I was not on the base! Here was an instance when I wanted to melt into the crowd, and now I could pass for an Aussie, or a Brit, or a New Zealander, or a French businessman.

Carefully I looked around. There were about fifteen other people eating lunch on the terrace. The American dignitaries were seated in such a way that a ring of empty tables served as a buffer around them, but I was actually quite surprised to see the lack of security provided them. We had not been asked to go inside and leave the terrace to the "top brass." The bodyguards were not wearing suit coats and I could see no evidence of any firearms. Perhaps a hastily arranged lunch had left no time for advance warning, but my military intelligence training flagged the possibility of danger.

By this time our lunch had arrived. The waiter poured two glasses of wine and left. I sat across from Thérèse, the VIPs conversing quietly in my left peripheral vision. It was all I could do to maintain eye contact with Thérèse while we talked. Bits and pieces of conversation from the adjacent table filtered into my consciousness. For example, they all ordered unsweet-ened iced tea.

I heard things like "How was your trip?" "Today is unusually hot," "Lyndon said," "My wife told me to. . . ."

The entire conversation sounded like pretty bor-ing stuff to me. Until the unsweetened iced teas arrived.

I had just taken a bite of my sandwich when I became aware that someone was approaching our table. I looked up to see Robert McNamara standing next to me.

"Are you finished with your sugar?" he asked.

He cut an imposing figure, though I did my best not to register recognition or surprise.

"*Pardon?*" I inquired in French.

Cool and collected I turned to Thérèse and asked in French, "What does he want?"

She, ever alert and ready for fun, picked up my cue and replied, "*Le sucre.*"

Here was a woman who wore her savvy well and rose to every occasion like a champ!

I looked at McNamara and said, "*O, oui! oui!*"

I handed him the sugar bowl and he returned to his table.

What a sweet victory this was! It was obvious that he didn't have a clue that I was a 2nd Lieutenant in the United States Army. I had completely bluffed the Secre-tary of Defense. Thérèse stared at me in total admiration, thunderstruck that I had had "the balls" to pull this one off. She couldn't stop talking about what I had done.

When we got back in her car she gave me a big kiss and exclaimed loudly, "I love you! I love you!"

"Me too," I mumbled. "I love you too."

But far more than Thérèse, I loved the fact that I had finally gotten one over on the military/civilian establishment.

Chapter 16
September, 1966

An Angry Seoul Brother

The Korean units sent to Vietnam to assist the United States were an elite fighting force. They were fierce fighters who understood the Asian mind of their Viet Cong and NVA adversaries. The VC/NVA were terrified of the Koreans, and tried valiantly to avoid engaging them in battle. One message that we intercepted from a VC headquarters to subordinate units concerned the rules of engagement with Korean troops. This communiqué listed ten rules of engagement, only five of which I can recall:

1. Make sure that you outnumber the Koreans at least ten to one.

2. Make sure that you have superior firepower.

3. Attack only at night.

4. Infiltrate and test the Korean's perimeter at least three times.

5. Do not take any prisoners. Execute any wounded.

As soldiers we often joked that the quickest way to end the Vietnam War would be to "train half of the Korean army in Hawaii under Israeli officers." All the U.S. would have to do would be to put up the money. No American soldiers, sailors, airmen, or marines would ever have to set foot on Vietnamese soil! But, unfortunately, the high command never listened to us.

All of the Korean soldiers in Vietnam had volunteered to serve there. They received extra pay, better food, and better weapons than the soldiers serving back home. However, the biggest advantage lay in their PX privileges. Each Korean soldier was issued a PX card identical to the ones issued to Americans. They could buy electronic equipment, clothing, personal hygiene products, and sundry other items at the main PX in Saigon, a store about as big as one of today's Wal-Marts. The Koreans responded like kids in a candy store. One item of a kind was never enough, a situation that irritated the heck out of me because the PX was constantly out of supplies that I needed. The Koreans were especially fond of Banlon polyester golf shirts. I recall seeing one Korean leaving the PX with at least thirty shirts slung over his shoulder. The shirts were used as currency with the local whores or occasionally were sent home as gifts.

Finally I was given an opportunity to use my Vietnamese language training in a military context. I had been asked to serve on a joint interrogation team with a Korean, a Vietnamese, an Australian, and a New Zealander. We were generally flown in by helicopter to a battle site after the shooting had ended and the prisoners had been blindfolded and tagged. We would then perform our interrogations. Prisoners who did not talk willingly were usually handled by the Korean, Sgt. Pak. He was a forceful man whose interrogation methods no one dared question and I can honestly say that during the entire time I served on the joint interrogation team, I never saw a prisoner tortured or abused. I always turned my back!

Eventually Sgt. Pak and I became close friends. He spoke excellent English as well as Vietnamese, had come from an upper middle class Korean family, and had graduated from a university in Korea. He had also spent one year in the United States doing research on Eskimo cultures. Pak had a wicked sense of humor and I could be reduced to spasms of laughter merely by watching him laugh. Pak and I gradually became die-hard drinking buddies and I introduced him to several of the mamasans that I knew. Pak had an insatiable weakness for Vietnamese women and crammed as much sexual activity as he could possibly muster into his busy days. I don't believe that Pak ever went into a bar without sampling at least one bar girl.

On one occasion when the joint interrogation team had just finished a full day at a battle site near Hue, Pak and I decided to go into the city, get dinner, and rent a decent hotel room for the night. The other members of the team hitched a ride with a transport plane heading back toward Saigon about 650 miles south. Pak and I walked out to the nearest road and hailed a taxi.

"Take us to Hue's central market," I told the driver.

Hue was known to the Vietnamese people as "the beautiful city," and not just because the most attractive people were said to come from there, or that it was considered the culinary center of central Vietnam. As the ancient capital of Vietnam, Hue provided the finest examples of two-hundred-year-old imperial architecture, dozens of pagodas and temples, and was inhabited by a very gentle people who liked Americans. During the winter months, the smells of thyme and oil trees filled the air, and in April the aroma of lotus blossoms provided a heady backdrop to the daily rounds of workday activity. Hue cafés at night were alive with people who enjoyed life and camaraderie.

During the mid 1960s, Hue had become the epicenter of protest against the regime of Nguyen Van Thieu in Saigon. Later Hue, located about 400 miles from Hanoi, became a stronghold of the North Vietnamese Army. During the Tet Offensive in January and February 1968, American artillery and, later, the South Vietnamese Air Force unfortunately destroyed much of the city and its architectural heritage.

Because the city was built around the Perfume River, the lives of the people revolved around this famous river. Houseboats, junks, and fishing boats were everywhere. The daily fish catch was legendary and the restaurant menus were predominantly fish dishes. Pak and I literally had our choice of five hundred restaurants where we could eat!

When we arrived at the central market, we wandered past a hodgepodge of vendors selling fresh produce, fish, meat, 8-track tapes, books, clothing, and souvenirs—anything to which a price tag could be attached. As we walked out onto the main street, the pungent smells of ethnic foods, the sight of exotic clothing, and a sea of pedicabs, cycles, and motorbikes greeted us. Hundreds of schoolgirls riding bicycles and dressed in their white "áo dài," the Vietnamese national dress, thronged the streets. They proudly showed off their "tóc thế," the traditional long flowing hair, and they all wore "nón bài tho'," a conical straw hat with a poem written inside that could only be read when held up to the light. Suddenly, I was *"Alex* in Wonderland," a foreign soldier jettisoned into an unreal world millions of miles removed from the War and my own country.

Eventually Pak and I wandered into a restaurant where a waiter showed us to a table that overlooked the Perfume River. We asked him to recommend a meal that had a specifically local flavor and he brought us a heaping dish of "cao lau," fried shrimp wontons with pineapple sauce. The main course was "bún bò Huế," Hue-style beef noodles and "tôm chua Huế, Hue sour shrimp, a dish both Pak and I liked so much that we ate the same thing for dinner all five nights that we stayed in Hue.

We also asked the waiter to recommend a hotel in town where we could stay. He wrote a name and address on a napkin, and we took a taxi to an old French hotel distinguished by its elegant foyer. We checked in, took a shower, and headed back down to the lobby. It was now time to sample Hue's vibrant nightlife.

We headed out into the night, turned to the left, and randomly began to wander along the busy streets. Many twists and turns later, we found the nightclub district and were soon invited into a club by a very beautiful lady soliciting business at the door. Once inside we sat at a long highly-polished wooden bar, the only non-Vietnamese customers in the establishment. I ordered bourbon and water and Pak ordered a Japanese Kirin beer while together we watched the bar girls "work" their Vietnamese customers. Within five minutes, two attractive Vietnamese women, whom I will call Mai #1 and Mai #2, approached us. Mai #1 began to chat with Pak, while Mai #2 moved in my direction.

We made the usual small talk. What's your name? How long had I been in Vietnam? Where had I learned the language? When I agreed to buy Mai #2 a Saigon tea, her interest in me seemed to perk up. (Of course, I was an American with money and I spoke her language!) In the background, I could hear Pak negotiating the night's stand with Mai #1. He felt that he should get a discount because he would supply the room; he was also concerned about venereal disease. Was Mai #1 "clean"? Indignantly, she swore up and down that she did not have "the clap," but Pak persisted and must have elicited four or five assurances from Mai #1 before the two of them agreed on a price and a location. Finally they left the bar arm in arm.

Mai #2 and I continued to talk and enjoy each other's company. Four or five teas later, Mai #2 asked me why I had not yet propositioned her. I said that I was in no hurry and, besides, I didn't think "she would be any good in bed." To her, this was a direct attack on her honor. She began to hurl insults at me claiming that I probably wasn't big enough to satisfy her. She reached down to grab my crotch.

"I feel you have too small for me," she smiled coquettishly.

Obviously, the girl found me attractive and was eager to earn my American dollars. Would such a challenge make me want to prove her wrong?

"It's not the pen that counts; it's the penmanship," I assured her.

My virility in question, I was now intent on preserving my macho image.

She laughed and made me an offer that I could not refuse. She would "service" me and, if I did not find her competent, there would be no charge. However, if I was honest with her and felt that she was indeed competent, I would pay double. I nodded my agreement, paid my bar bill, and we left. Halfway back to the hotel, we ran into Pak and Mai #1. The smiles on their faces told the story!

"See you back at the bar in an hour or so," I called over my shoulder.

In a nutshell, Mai #2 was "hotter than a half-fucked fox in a forest fire." When I asked her how she had become so competent, her response took me totally off guard.

"I believe in spirit of old world craftsman." I laughed at the absurdity of her words.

"Where on earth did you ever pick up that bit of wisdom?" I inquired.

This certainly was not an expression response I would have expected to hear from a local whore on the back streets of Hue.

"My boyfriend tell me that. He now dead." she told me in her best broken English.

At this point I wasn't so sure that *she* hadn't screwed him to death! But I saw the sadness in her eyes and made no further comment.

Mai #2 and I returned to the bar where I took my leave of Pak and the two ladies. I was ready to call it a night after a rather remarkable and unexpected interlude on the back streets of Hue. This country of vast contrasts in people, culture, and terrain never ceased to amaze and challenge me. I was drawn to this place in such a way that I felt like an integral part of the Vietnamese people and their suffering. As I returned to my hotel, I promised myself that I would someday return regardless of which regime was in place.

For the next three days Pak and I concentrated on touring the city. We climbed to ancient tombs, traipsed through imperial palaces, roamed through incredible temples, investigated ornate pagodas, and visited various places of interest around the area. Every evening, however, we returned exhausted to the stark realities of war. Sounds of artillery bombardment outside the city shattered any pleasurable excitement of our day. The suburbs of Hue, known to be active North Vietnamese Army operational areas, provided a grim reminder that we were indeed at war. Each morning, we checked in by telephone with our superiors in Saigon to get an update on our situation. And every morning we were told to "sit tight" and wait for further instructions. That was fine with us!

On the morning of the third day, I heard Pak moaning in the bathroom. When he came out I asked him what was going on. He swore up a storm and told me that, every time he urinated, he experienced a severe burning sensation accompanied by a small discharge. Well aware of what the problem might be, I suggested that he see a military doctor and get a diagnosis. He agreed, and together we took off for the US Army medical detachment stationed in Hue. The diagnosis was immediate: bacterial urethritis, "the clap." The doctor gave Pak a shot of penicillin and a ten-day supply of Tetracycline.

Pak was angry, to say the least. He kept inquiring if I had any symptoms similar to his, and I responded "No." At times he seemed upset that I had avoided his problem: "Why me, not Pete?" That afternoon Pak told me that he wanted to go back to the bar where he had met Mai #1 and let her know that she needed to seek medical attention.

A nice thing to do, I thought. He wanted to run a few errands, but said that he would be at the bar at around 6:00 P.M. and I could catch up with him then.

I arrived at the bar at 6:10 P.M., a mere ten minutes late. When I walked in, Pak and Mai #1 were in the throes of a heated argument in a far corner of the room. Fingers were pointed, accusations flew, and a small crowd

of bar girls, eager to be in on the latest news, had clus-
tered around the two combatants. Mai #1 screamed at
the top of her lungs that Pak had given her venereal disease; Pak, for his part, responded that the situation was
just the opposite. I could see that Pak was losing his cool.
He reached into his front pocket, pulled out something
that looked like baling wire, and grabbed Mai #1 by the
blouse. He threw her to the ground and sat on her legs.
He proceeded to take off her slacks and pull down her
panties.

The terrified woman fought to escape, but Pak had
her pretty well pinned on the ground. Sensing the danger
of the situation, I jumped in to pull him away—but was
punched so hard in the stomach that I staggered and fell
to the ground. Regaining my balance, I reentered the
fray. Pak had a loop of the stiff wire in his hand and was
trying to do something between Mai #1's legs. I couldn't
believe my eyes! PAK WAS TRYING TO SEW UP HER
VAGINA WITH WIRE!!!

Finally, the screaming and commotion attracted the
attention of passers-by who notified the police. Within
minutes, four "white mice" (Vietnamese National Police
who wore white uniforms and drove Harley-Davidson
motorcycles) arrived. They used their nightsticks to sub-
due Pak, who now, outmatched, stood up and tried to run.
The police tripped and quickly handcuffed Pak, and led
him away to a nearby police van which sped off down the
street.

I hailed a pedicab and told the driver to take me to
the nearest police station. When I inquired about Sgt.
Pak, the sergeant at the desk told me that no one had
been brought in. He suggested that I try the police station
about three miles further down the road. When I arrived
there, they also had no knowledge of the incident. Pak

had disappeared! Where in the hell had they taken him? I had to know.

I went back to the bar. The mamasan politely asked me to leave and begged me not to return. The assembled girls shouted insults and refused to talk. I could not locate Mai #1. Finally, in a state of total confusion and disbelief, I returned to my hotel room. There I collapsed on the bed and began to sob quietly. My buddy Pak had entered a state of "temporary invisibility." What could I possibly do? Eventually, unable to calm myself, I left the room and wandered aimlessly up and down the streets of Hue, gazing mindlessly in shop windows, and trying to compose myself. When I returned to the room several hours later, all of Pak's belongings were gone! He had literally vanished into thin air.

The next morning I called my superior in Saigon and asked if he had heard about Pak's situation. He told me that Pak was already headed back to Korea on a military transport plane and that he was facing a court-martial for his actions. He also told me that the court-martial would be a "show trial" to appease the Vietnamese authorities. Pak would probably be returned to duty in Korea after some perfunctory punishment had been meted out.

"Is there anything I can do, Sir? Be a witness for the defense? Visit him for moral support?" I pleaded. I still couldn't believe that all this had happened within such a short period of time.

The resounding "No" on the other end of the line nearly shattered my eardrums.

"Fournier, get the hell back there ASAP. If your ass isn't in my office by 0900, I'm feeding you to the Korean dogs. Head back to base NOW!"

And to my mind, sooner was better!

Field Manual 22-67

I had just been promoted to the rank of 1st Lieutenant and assigned as the Executive Officer of the 175th RRC. One morning I was sitting at my desk contemplating the meaning of life and picking my teeth when I noticed a large pile of Army Field Manuals in the corner. There must have been over 100 of these manuals. I picked one up. It was about small engine repair. Another one was about embalming techniques. There seemed to be a manual on just about every military subject you could imagine. As I ran through the pile, I noticed that there was one glaring weakness. There was no manual about how to deal with a WAC (Women's Army Corps). That wasn't fair. WACs were everywhere, and an important part of our military strength. So, I decided to write the first manual on how to operate a U.S. WAC. I borrowed a typewriter from the Company clerk and began to type. The result is shown on the following pages.

FM 22-67

THE U.S. WAC

M-1 MODEL 1966

JANUARY 1967

1. <u>GENERAL CHARACTERISTICS</u>:   The U.S. WAC is designed as a auxiliary weapon to the U.S. BED, M-3 MODEL 1776. It is mouth fed, recoil operated, air-cooled, and can be activated in any position and at any elevation.

2. <u>NOMENCLATURE AND OPERATION</u>:   The WAC (average) has an overall length of 62 inches. The circumference varies with the age of the weapon. The WAC is equipped with two cushioned projectiles on the front of the weapon, and each can be used as a handhold during operation. The breach, the most important part, is located between the sockets of the ambulatory limbs. The ambulatory limbs allow the WAC to be mobile when not in actual operation. The breach is discussed in detail in Section 3 of this manual.

3. <u>NOMENCLATURE OF THE BREACH</u>:   The breach of the U.S. WAC is composed of three (3) main groups. The first, the fur cover, is not essential and some gunners prefer the U.S. WAC Breach Model M-2, which has no cover. The second group is the breach projection lips. The breach projection lips are elastic and, during operation, open to allow entrance of the projectile. The breach projection lips are designed to fit snugly against the sides of the projectile during the firing sequence. The breach proper has an opening that expands to accommodate a projectile of up to 150 caliber. The length of the projectile is not critical. The breach proper is equipped with an internal lubrication device that keeps the bore well oiled during firing. Periodic adjustments and cleaning are automatic functions of the lubrication device that render the weapon inoperable during this period.

4. <u>CARE AND CLEANING</u>: This topic need not be discussed here since all of these details are cared for by

the WAC, the Quartermaster Corps, the Ordinance De-
pot, and the Kimberly-Clark Corporation. (See FM
22-60, the U.S. Sanitary Napkin, M-5).

5. OPERATION AND FIRING OF THE U.S. WAC, M-1, MODEL 1966:

a. The weapon is best operated by a single gunner. Since the gunner may be easily fatigued
while operating the weapon, crews may work in
rotation. A special precaution, though, is to allow not more than five (5) crews per one firing.

b. Position of the gunner and his function during the firing:

The gunner places himself between the ambulatory limbs of the WAC, with the projectile held
firmly in his right hand. On the first count, the
gunner drops to a kneeling position, and, at the
same time braces himself with his left hand. The
projectile is placed against the breach projection lips, and the gunner places his head between the cushioned projectiles.

c. Operation:

To place the weapon into operation the command is:

"Wiggle Damn Ya!" On the command of ex-
ecution, the gunner forces the projectile into
the breach and immediately begins rhythmic
perturbations until the shell explodes. The
empty shell casing is withdrawn and the gunner moves to the prone position on either
side of the weapon, and rests while the
weapon cools and the shell is reloaded.

6. <u>SPECIAL CONDITIONS</u>: After the gunner becomes proficient in the operation of the WAC, he may use his own variations of firing. Special attention is brought to the fact that the weapon is equally capable of indoor and outdoor firing. The prescribed firing position is horizontal, but many variations may be used.

7. <u>STOPPAGES</u>: After the gun is put into action, stoppage rarely, if ever occurs. However, in some cases it may be difficult to place the projectile in the breach before firing. The field expedient in this case is to hand operate the breach until the self-lubricating mechanism is activated. Any other stoppage will have to be left to the gunner to correct.

8. <u>SURPLUS SALES</u>: Though the U.S. WAC, M-1, MODEL 1966 is normally discharged when it becomes inoperative or surplus, they may be found available after return to civilian life by many of the gunners who have learned their operation and wish to continue after their own discharge from the service. In case one can not be found when needed, reasonable facsimiles can usually be found walking the streets after dark.

BY ORDER OF:

William S. Twatley
OIC, US 1

OFFICIAL:

Vernon J. Putz
OIC, US 12

DISTRIBUTION:
  As Requested*

Chapter 18
January 1967

Joy to the World

Most of the 400 men of the 175th RRC worked in an air-conditioned cinderblock building called White Birch on the outskirts of Saigon. The roof of this building bristled with antennas and other communications equipment. The workday was divided into three shifts: 8:00 A.M.–4:00 P.M.; 4:00 P.M.–midnight; and midnight–8:00 A.M.

SP5 Thomas Billings worked the midnight to 8:00 A.M. shift. Tom was a hard-working kid from Iowa who enlisted in the Army to get away from the family hog farm. In November of 1963, Tom took the oath and joined the United States Army Security Agency in the only **four-year** enlistment option offered in the US Army. What Tom didn't know at the time was that bureaucratic confusion would change his life forever.

It was in the same month that Tom joined the Army (November, 1963) that the enlistment period for the USASA was changed from a three-year commitment to a four-year commitment. As I came to find out later, there were always 10% of the recruiters who never "got the word." This was the case with the Army personnel clerks who processed PVT Billings' enlistment paperwork. Some of the documents reflected a three-year enlistment and some reflected a four-year enlistment. The Army had accidentally invented a hybrid 3½-year tour of duty!

Tom went his merry way. He did his basic training at Ft. Jackson, SC, and then was assigned to Ft. Devens, MA for intelligence training. Tom was sent to 98C training, Communications Traffic Analysis. During his entire basic training and technical training phases, no one in Army personnel noticed Tom's mixed enlistment paperwork. Even when Tom got his orders for a two-year assignment to Bad Aibling, Germany and was out- processed from Ft. Devens, the discrepancy remained unnoticed.

In August 1966, SP5 Tom Billings returned to the States after two years in Germany, having served about thirty-three months of his current enlistment. As far as Tom knew, he had fifteen months left in the Army. Tom took thirty days of leave and then reported to the National Security Agency at Ft. Meade, Maryland. As it turned out, there was no permanent position for Tom's MOS (Military Occupational Specialty) at NSA. Thus, in the middle of November, Tom was informed that he had been reassigned for a one-year tour of duty to the 175th RRC in Vietnam to finish his enlistment. Apparently, the Army personnel clerks who processed Tom's assignment were using the four-year information in his personnel files.

Early in December 1966, Tom arrived in Vietnam and reported to the Commanding Officer, Captain Whitman, at the 175th RRC. Tom was processed-in, given his housing assignment, and put on the midnight to 8:00 A.M. shift at Operations. He was also introduced to me,

2nd Lt. Pete Fournier, the Assistant Executive Officer. Tom's personnel file was taken from him by the Company Clerk and later sent to the personnel detachment at Battalion headquarters in Long Bien. Tom settled in for one final year of self-preservation.

My own military career was going well and on January 3, 1967, I was appointed Acting Executive Officer. It was only four days later that I received a phone call from W3 Hugh Leffler, Battalion Personnel Officer at Long Bien. He wanted to know if we had a SP5 Thomas Billings in the unit. I responded that we did. At this moment I thought that the phone line had gone dead.

And then I heard the thundering question: "What in the fuck is he doing there?"

Obviously, there was some problem way beyond my understanding at the moment.

I collected my thoughts and replied, "He's probably asleep in his rack, Mister. He works the midnight to 8:00 shift at Operations."

"Asleep in his rack? Goddamn it, Fournier! He's not even in the Army!"

He slammed some hard object on his desk to underscore his point. From twenty kilometers away I could feel his frustration.

"Excuse me, Mister," I began.

Now my curiosity was doing handstands. *How could someone be in the Army and not be in the Army at the same time?*

"I don't think I get your meaning," I mumbled.

Was I the one asleep in his rack?

"Let me repeat myself, Fournier. *He's not even in the Army!*"

The voice was loud, irritable, and resolute.

Exasperation and annoyance crackled on the other end of the phone. I had been in the Army long enough to know I shouldn't meddle with it.

Despite my better judgment, I sarcastically retorted, "Coulda fooled me, Mister. I saw him yesterday in the motor pool."

Leffler finally screamed. "You had better get your young ass up here this morning. We've got a big problem!"

I moved my 'young ass' ASAP. I borrowed a jeep from the motor pool and headed for Long Bien. When I arrived at Battalion Headquarters, Leffler was waiting for me at the front door. He was highly agitated, walking in circles and whimpering something about his career being "shot in the ass." He took my arm and pushed me into a small room just off the entryway into the building. The room was windowless and had a small round table placed in the center with three office chairs around it. I immediately spotted a thick brown manila folder lying in the middle of the table.

Leffler boomed, "Sit down, Lieutenant" and pulled out one of the chairs for me.

He remained standing and ordered me to open the folder. Written on the cover was "Billings, Thomas, RA 13******." The large packet contained two other folders, one labeled "1963" and one labeled "1964." As I paged through the two folders it became clear to me that there were duplicate forms and correspondence that showed discharge dates of *November 9, 1963* and *November 9, 1964.*

"Holy shit, what do we do now?" was my instant reaction.

Definitely this situation was one I could never have imagined in my wildest dreams.

"You got me by the short hairs," replied Leffler.

We both remained frozen in place; dumb looks smeared helplessly across our befuddled faces.

The mood was broken by a knock on the door.

"Come in," bellowed Leffler.

Slowly the door opened and Major Bill Hartman entered.

"What are you guys doing in here?" he asked in surprise. "I've got a meeting scheduled in this room in ten minutes."

"Sir, you wouldn't believe it even if I told you," replied Leffler.

By this time the Battalion Personnel officer was beginning to show signs of wear.

"We have a situation here that's way beyond anything I can figure out."

"Tell me anyway," Hartman ordered.

Leffler took a deep breath and quickly tried to explain the complicated problem.

Major Hartman struck me as a take-charge guy and he didn't let me down.

"Well, it seems that this situation needs to be resolved NOW," Hartman affirmed. "There are three of us here right now. Let's take a vote. Everyone in favor of November 9, 1963, raise your hand."

I raised my hand and waited. Major Hartman looked over his shoulder toward the open door, went over and closed it, and raised his hand. When Leffler saw that he was the odd man out, he slowly raised his hand.

"Well, I guess it's unanimous," Hartman announced. "Leffler, I'm putting you in charge of getting the paperwork in order. Fournier, you're responsible for seeing to it that Thomas Billings is on the next plane out of the country this afternoon."

I slumped back in my chair, emotionally drained. Never before had I dealt with such life-altering decisions in such a short span of time.

As I sped back to Tan Son Nhut, I was relieved and excited. It had been truly refreshing to see an officer take a sticky situation by the horns and resolve it on the spot. Not since basic training had I seen an individual of any rank act so decisively. But now I needed to devise a plan for getting SP5 Thomas Billings out of the country today. I looked at my watch. It was noon.

I arrived back in the company area at about 12:30 P.M. I immediately raced to my office and told the Company clerk to come in and shut the door. I explained the situation to PFC Dowling as succinctly as possible.

His reaction was typical, "Holy shit, Sir. What do we do now?"

"Dowling, if you can pull off the out-processing and flight arrangements by the end of the day, I'll authorize an R&R to Bangkok."

His eyes lit up like two laser beams. Since he had already been on one R&R to Hong Kong, this was an opportunity he couldn't pass up!

He jumped up, let out a yell, and exclaimed, "Consider it done, Sir, or my name isn't 'Whateverittakes' Dowling."

I smiled broadly because I knew that he would find a way! If not, he would really let me, Billings, and the Major down. As I left the orderly room, I asked a passing soldier if he knew where I could find SP5 Billings.

"C-Building," he responded as I turned to make a quick beeline in that direction.

C-Building was reserved for soldiers on the midnight to 8:00 A.M. shift so that they could sleep during the day without interruption. The barracks was built on stilts that elevated it approximately three feet off the ground and had louvered sides lined with screening. At both the front and back of the building were two large pedestal fans that blew lukewarm air down the center aisle. Each building had two rows of twenty-five double bunks. Both the upper and lower bunks were rigged with mosquito netting and each double bunk had associated with it a small wardrobe for two men and two footlockers. The men were able to fashion cubicles of sorts using the wardrobe and foot-lockers as partitions.

It was 1:15 P.M. when I walked up the steps of C-Building and opened the door. I could see that there were about thirty exhausted men sleeping quietly. As I walked down the aisle, I noticed that the third cubicle on the right had a footlocker marked "BILLINGS." Asleep in the bottom rack was Thomas. He looked so cherubic sleeping on top of his sheets, dressed only in a pair of olive drab boxer shorts.

I bent over, gently tapped him on the shoulder, and whispered, "Billings, get up."

On the third "Billings, get up," he opened his eyes and tried to focus on my face and the black rank bar on my camouflage uniform.

"Sir, what do you want?"

Billings sat up and turned to face me.

Groggily he repeated, "Sir, what do you want?"

I said, "Billings, I want you to get up, stuff your things in a duffel bag, and get the hell out of here!"

"Why do you want me to do that, Sir?"

I looked Thomas Billings squarely in the eye and exclaimed, "Because you're out of the Army!!!"

"What? What are you talking about, Sir?"

I took a deep breath and, as rapidly as my lips could spew out the words, I yelled "The Army made a mistake. you're out of the Army! The Army made a mistake. you're out of the Army!"

At this point I first noticed that a small crowd had formed.

The curious onlookers began mindlessly chanting, "He's out of the Army. He's out of the Army."

All of a sudden Thomas Billings realized that, maybe just maybe, he wasn't dreaming. He slid out of his bunk, leapt into the air, and began crying, yelling, hugging, and kissing people all at the same time. He jumped into my arms and began kissing the top of my head, my cheeks, and my ears. He turned around and began hugging and kissing anyone within six feet of him.

I yelled, "Start packing before the Army changes its mind!"

Eager well-wishers began helping Thomas stuff his clothing and issue items into a duffel bag. Thomas was so disoriented that he took off his boxer shorts, threw them into the air, and then put them back on. He was just barely able to assemble a uniform with boots and socks before everything was stuffed into his duffel bag. He ran out of the building and began accosting people in the company area with more hugs, kisses, and war whoops.

At 3:30 P.M., a jeep pulled into the company area to pick up SP5 Thomas Billings and take him to the Tan Son Nhut airport terminal for boarding of a 4:00 P.M. flight headed to the Oakland Army Terminal in California. My last view of Thomas Billings was of him jumping up and down in the back seat of the jeep as it pulled away. I felt a little like Jesus must have felt when he told Lazarus to rise from the dead.

I never asked PFC Dowling how he made the impossible happen. Not unexpectedly, the next day this poor Company Clerk was overwhelmed by 400 requests from soldiers wanting to have *their* Personnel Records checked.

As promised, the following month PFC Dowling got his week to rest and recuperate in Bangkok.

Chapter 19
July 1967

Oink!

Our Company unit was called the 175th RRC (Radio Research Company). If any of the locals asked what we did there, the standard response was always "We research radios." I always derived a sort of perverse pleasure in receiving a truly dumb look: "What the hell is this guy talking about?"

A radio is a radio is a radio, or so thought the curious questioner who eyed our communications system from every available angle and waited for our reaction. "No kidding," we'd declare! "We take radios apart to see what makes them tick." More often than not, our puzzled locals would move away to the more important duties of daily survival. But we were never totally sure that they fell for our simplistic explanations.

The truth of the matter was we were a field station of the Army Security Agency, a subordinate to the National Security Agency (NSA) at Ft. Meade, MD. All of us were highly trained in communications intelligence. Our job was to intercept North Vietnamese, Viet Cong, and Cambodian military communications, decode and translate the intercept, then analyze the plain text prior to reporting pertinent information to our Headquarters in Arlington Hall Station, Virginia and to NSA.

The Company area was located adjacent to the main runway at Tan Son Nhut airport and was only a stone's throw from the main hangars. The compound looked and felt "state-side," with wooded louvered-wall buildings, an NCO club, a shower and toilet building, an old colonial fifty-seat theater, and even a decrepit tennis court. Everyone slept in one of five elevated, screened-in barracks with a wooden floor. We vied for toilet privileges and discovered that, usually before you could use the facilities, you had to wipe sandaled footprints from the seat. Our Vietnamese houseboys and yardmen had not quite mastered the art of positioning one's butt on a Western toilet!

And then there was OINK, the pride and joy of the 175th RRC! Rumor had it that a GI whose father owned a pig farm in Kansas had rescued this beagle pooch from the streets of Saigon and had named the dog accordingly. Whatever the case, Oink reigned supreme as the uncontested survivor of numerous military, canine, and vehicular encounters. A grizzled veteran of back-alley conquests, he at some point had been run over by a car and had lost his right hind leg. No matter! Oink could out-maneuver the best of us and managed to move from point A to point B with relative ease. His one weakness? An apparent "allergic" reaction to the hot, moist air of Saigon's long sweltering summer! On these torrid days he spent most of his time stretched out in the deep-purple shade beneath the barracks nearest the mess hall. Oink also reveled in his self-appointed role as the "King's Taster" of military rations. Each day like clockwork, he'd leave his shaded patch and slowly amble to the mess hall where he'd lay in wait near the exit. And, each day like clockwork, the troops doled out scraps as they filed through the chow line. For months this routine went on until gradually, a 175th RRC tradition was established: the first GI through the chow line would throw Oink a scrap from his meal. If Oink turned his nose up at the food, the chow was fit for human consumption. If Oink ate the scrap, we all abandoned the mess hall and headed for the NCO club! In this way, Oink was ceremoniously credited with saving many a hungry soldier from the ravages of diarrhea, vomiting, and stomach cramps.

I was the duty officer one afternoon when two enlisted men came into my office. Obviously concerned about something important, they hemmed and hawed, exchanging awkward glances in an effort to get the problem off their chests.

"What's eating you guys?" I asked. "You both look like the cat that ate the canary, yet you're acting more like the cat's got your tongues. Spit it out!"

The afternoon heat had chipped away at my patience and left me short on tolerance, long on my need to close up shop.

"Well Sir! It's hard to explain, but Oink is whimpering, licking his dick over and over, and he won't come out from under the barracks."

The first soldier pushed his buddy forward to finish what he had started.

"And we're worried that he may have eaten something that he shouldn't have. "He's looking mighty pale."

The two men obviously had Oink's welfare at heart, leading me to share a measure of their concern. Since I was a commissioned officer, it was up to me to come up with a quick solution.

"I have an idea, gentlemen." I leaned forward as a resolution came into focus. "Why not," I suggested, "take Oink up the street to the 1455th USAF Veterinary Detachment? The airmen and vets at the clinic are responsible for taking care of all the German Shepherds that patrol the perimeter of Tan Son Nhut. See if they can help." I took a note pad and quickly penned a request.

One of the soldiers blurted out, "Hey, this is kinda neat. Almost like a medical referral."

I sat back satisfied that I had at least proposed a plausible way around the problem. The two enlisted guys agreed that this was a logical plan of attack. So, with a hot dog "borrowed" from the mess hall in hand, they lured the unsuspecting Oink out from under the barracks and hoisted him into the back seat of a jeep.

Two hours later the squeal of rubber and the screech of jamming brakes jarred me from my duties. The jeep transporting Oink and the two GIs bounced into the center of the Company area and came to a noisy halt. In the midst of this god-awful racket the two "Samaritans," their patient in tow, had returned from their mission. Even from a distance I could tell that something unexpected was in the mix. The driver wore a grin from ear to ear; the passenger was doubled over in the seat and laughing uncontrollably.

In the meantime, word had spread throughout the unit that Oink had been carted off to the vets. By the time the medical expedition had returned, every soldier within hearing distance had congregated to get the scoop.

"Hey, what's wrong with Oink?" one anxious onlooker demanded.

The crowd pushed closer, all eyes on the jeep and its occupants, all ears cocked to hear what ailed their beleaguered dog. A wave of silent anticipation washed over those assembled!

Then suddenly the driver stood on the back seat and broadcast in a bellowing voice: "The CLAP! OINK'S GOT THE CLAP!!! They gave him a shot and we gotta give him this 'tetracycling' for his gonorrhea three times a day."

Gleefully, the soldier brandished a small prescription envelope high above his head.

A mighty cheer erupted from the crowd. Soldiers flipped their hats into the air, waved their arms uproariously, and dropped to the ground in spasms of laughter.

Shouts of "Oink's one of us!" rose above the din and hung tenaciously in the afternoon heat.

It was not surprising that such a commotion caught the attention of Company Commander, Captain Robinson James Whitman. A straight laced, highly unpopular "leader of men," Whitman burst from the dayroom with vengeance on his mind.

"What the fuck is going on here?" he bellowed.

Goose-stepping straight toward me, he deftly backed me against a wall and eyeballed me from a lethal one-millimeter vantage point.

Again he screamed in my face, "You heard me! What the fuck's going on here, Fournier? You're supposed to be in charge!"

His contorted features were now redder than a freshly spanked buttock. Sucking in my breath, I struggled to remain calm.

"The troops are celebrating a momentous occasion, Sir. Oink's back from the vet. They're merely having a bit of fun." Whitman's "Huh?" made it very clear, however, that my lame explanation was having little effect.

Suddenly one of the men on the perimeter of the crowd yelled "Oink's got balls! That's more than we can say about some of the officers around here."

Whitman's face turned livid as he spun in rage and strained to see who had hurled the insult. The offending soldier, however, had melted mysteriously into the crowd. Sensing a full-blown war within a war, I suggested that Whitman accompany me to his office where I would attempt to explain the situation that was unraveling as we spoke. This saved the day. Whitman wheeled abruptly and marched into the dayroom where he promptly disappeared into his office. I was right behind.

With nerves on edge and a heart racing faster than I care to remember, I moved toward the chair in front of the desk. Nothing looked better to me at this point than the welcoming support of that old wooden chair!

"Fournier, stand at attention when I speak to you!" Whitman ordered. The fire in his eyes left no doubt that he meant business. "Now, I want to know exactly what's got this place in such an uproar."

"Sir," I responded smartly, "A couple of guys thought that Oink was under the weather, so I had them take him up to the 1455th. Well, it seems that Oink has some kind of VD or urethral problem."

In my wildest dreams I could not imagine how this story was going to fly . . . but I continued on. Whitman's eyes grew buggier and buggier until I thought that his carotid arteries were going to burst.

"I'll tell you this and I'll tell you *once* only. You had better get to the bottom of this or your ass is mine."

By now Commander Whitman was in a full-blown rage and angling for a piece of my butt.

"But, Sir," I assured him. "*I* didn't give Oink the clap!"

Whitman pulled himself up to his full six-foot, two-hundred-fifty pounds.

"I don't give a flying fuck. If the Colonel ever finds out about this, I'll be breaking rocks at Leavenworth. Now get the fuck outta here and report back to me in the morning."

I saluted and hurriedly left the dayroom.

Obviously, Lieutenant Pete Fournier was not going to let this happen during his watch. I decided to investigate the Oink mystery by calling in my contacts. As a former SP5, I had made friends with the best enlisted buddies a man could ever want. Despite some good-natured abuse when I had been commissioned, my old barracks mates had never begrudged me my new position. Although Whitman had warned me several times that the officer corps frowned upon fraternizing with enlisted men, I had continued to drink and carouse with my friends—out of uniform and out of sight of the other commissioned officers.

So now I had a strategy. I requested Sgt. Forbes and Sgt. Kooper to stop by my office the next morning.

"Ask around," I instructed, "and see if you can find out how in the hell Oink could have contracted the clap."

Laughingly, they bought into the plan.

"But don't be obvious!" I cautioned, suddenly fearful that this could develop into the biggest news sweep of the year. I could just envision the staff of *Stars and Stripes* getting wind of this story.

It took only a few inquiries. Forbes and Kooper returned early the next morning with the following details:

> On the night of September 6th, Specialists Harriman and Bosworth were returning after an evening of carousing at the NCO club. As they staggered through the Company area, they spied a lonely silhouette in the distance. Low and behold, as they approached they recognized Oink standing in solitary splendor in the moonlight! Harriman stumbled up to Oink, threw his arms around the pooch and planted a big kiss on his furry forehead. Barely able to focus, Bosworth remarked, "Hey, everyone around here gets laid but Oink. Poor Oink." To this Harriman replied, "Hey dog, this is your lucky night!" A drunken plan had already begun to take shape in his mind.
>
> Harriman and Bosworth proceeded to put Oink in a Lambretta taxi and headed for downtown Saigon. At the notorious *Blue Heron* they negotiated with one of the prostitutes, who agreed to service Oink for 500 piasters or about $6.50.

I thanked Forbes and Kooper profusely and assured them that their account was secure with me. But now I was faced with taking some action based on the information I had received. "What in the hell does one do in such a situation?" I mused. I decided to confront Harriman and Bosworth in order to get their side of the story first-hand.

I sent the Company clerk out to get Harriman and Bosworth and bring them to my office. Immediately, from the looks on their faces, I could tell that they knew that I knew. They saluted and I told them to sit.

Before I could say anything Harriman squirmed in his chair and blurted out, "We were only having fun, Sir!" His earnest expression signaled a plea for understanding. "We certainly would never hurt Oink," Bosworth added.

Both men laughed sheepishly and in a nervous effort to convince me that the whole thing was a misguided prank.

"Tell that to Oink!" I thundered.

Though I had mustered my most authoritative tone, I had to bite my lip to keep from bursting into laughter at the absurdity of the situation.

"Don't you two idiots realize that each of you holds a Top Secret Crypto Clearance and that this behavior is not befitting an intelligent, professional soldier?"

They were incredulous that the Army would consider this prank anything but a practical joke. Eventually, however, the reality of their stupidity prevailed; they both admitted to a gross lapse in judgment and apologized profusely claiming alcoholic lunacy.

I was at a loss as to what punishment would fit this "crime." There were clear-cut penalties for stealing, lying, cheating, insubordination, and being AWOL. But there was nothing on the books for moral turpitude. I knew that I had to be creative! Thus, I gave each of them an Article 15 with confinement to base and revocation of NCO club privileges for 30 days with no forfeiture of pay. They were also tasked with giving Oink his twice-daily dose of tetracycline.

Oink, meanwhile, sailed into stardom. He was feted, cajoled, and paraded across the compound in a flurry of adulation. Toasted and hailed as a mascot unparalleled in this man's army, he happily accepted the hype and fanfare with a definitive wag of his stubby tail. These accolades were his undeniable due—all, that is, but the dreaded tetracycline pills! These he resisted with a mighty howl, demonstrating on several painful occasions that his BITE was indeed far worse than his BARK!

Chapter 20
August 1967

Fun with Money

In the early days of my service in Vietnam, a friend in the barracks introduced me to a Pakistani merchant who had been in the country for over twenty-five years. Mr. Lalchand owned a small tailor and retail-clothing store in one of the downtown buildings. He fashioned suits, pants, coats, shirts, and other custom-made apparel from massive bolts of fine cloth imported from England and beautiful silk from Thailand. He also sold a complete line of Angora sweaters imported from Turkey.

Lalchand was a dark-skinned, rotund man who wheezed heavily whenever he walked more than fifty feet. He was a childless widower who had cohabited with a Vietnamese lady for more than ten years. Lalchand's immediate family lived in Hong Kong and he regularly corresponded with his two brothers there. A shrewd and calculating merchant, Lalchand was the consummate Asian businessman.

I had known Lalchand for several months when I asked him what my price would be for six Angora sweaters to send home to my wife. He told me that he would give me twenty-five percent off, a deal to which I quickly agreed. I purchased them and sent them home for my wife's birthday. In a return letter, my wife raved about the sweaters and told me she had gotten many compliments from her coworkers. Subsequently, however, in a letter that I received a month later, she informed me that she had taken several sweaters to the dry cleaners and had discovered that they were 100% polyester. We were both crushed.

I confronted Lalchand who eventually "fessed up" to having duped me. I was furious and threatened to kill him on the spot. Actually, I was more hurt than angry because I felt Lalchand and I had become good friends. He refunded twice my money and promised never to cheat me again.

It was during this period that the United States introduced MPC (Military Payment Certificates). Green dollars were forbidden and the possession of US currency was considered a felony, punishable by court-martial. We were told that the Chinese government was acquiring green dollars in Vietnam and using the cash to purchase arms on the world market and from the Soviet Union. Thus, the flow of green dollars had to be halted. Replacing greenbacks with scrip was the logical first step. All soldiers were paid in MPC, and all military commerce (PX purchases, NCO Club purchases, etc.) was paid for in MPC. The military had established numerous locations in the city where one could convert MPC into Vietnamese piasters at the official rate. The usual rate during this period was 77 piasters per one-dollar MPC. The denomination of the MPC was irrelevant: it remained 77 to 1.

Green dollars, on the other hand, fluctuated on the black market. Lalchand entered the picture precisely because it was illegal for anyone to have green dollars; and,

Lalchand reigned as the largest moneychanger in all of Saigon and the surrounding countryside.

His operation was impressive! I once estimated that Lalchand laundered over $5,000 per day through his small store. Several months after I had first met him and when he had learned to trust me implicitly, I would sit in the back room behind a row of filing cabinets and listen to his transactions. There was a steady stream of customers. From Lalchand, the following exchange rate applied for greenbacks:

- one-dollar bill—85 piasters,
- five-dollar bill—500 piasters (100 piasters/dollar),
- ten-dollar bill—1,300 piasters,
- fifty-dollar bill—7,500 piasters,
- hundred-dollar bill—17,500 piasters (more than double the official rate).

Doubling one's money was easy. Just ask your wife or girlfriend to send you a weekly letter that contained a crisp $100 bill. Then take the bill to Lalchand and get 17,500 piasters for it. You could then walk down the street to the Bank of America and make a deposit into your savings account. When they did the conversion, your 17,500 piasters was worth a $227 deposit. One had to be careful to spread out their deposits so as to not raise any suspicions. The object was to be a minnow in a large pond. As long as one stayed well under the radar, one was not attracting any attention from the American authorities. I knew of officers who had tried to quadruple and quintuple their money all at once. I suspect they are still breaking rocks in Leavenworth!

The biggest problem for Lalchand, however, was getting the accumulated green dollars out of the country to Hong Kong. To this end, he had recruited a number of military personnel. When an individual was scheduled to go on an R & R to Hong Kong or to the resort city of Penang, Lalchand was willing to pay a five percent commission on any money smuggled into those locations by the travelers. Lalchand had also recruited several American military pilots to ferry money to Bangkok, Taipei, and Tokyo where he had other family members or relatives.

When I told Lalchand that I had applied for and received an R & R to Hong Kong, he was delirious. Over the years he had designed a series of money belts: one for around the waist, two for around the thighs, and two for around the calves. If one wore loose clothing over the money belts, it was then possible to smuggle money into the destination country. The commission on $50,000 was then about $2,500. This easily paid for the entire trip with some left over.

For my R & R to Hong Kong, Lalchand outfitted me with his finest set of belts. I was surprised how unobtrusive they were and how easily I could walk and move around hardly aware of what I was wearing. Lalchand had given me the name and phone number of one of his cousins who lived and worked in Hong Kong. I was to check into the President Hotel and then phone his cousin. The cousin would come over to the hotel, pick up the money, and "take care of me" for the rest of the week.

On the appointed day I boarded the R & R flight from Saigon to Hong Kong with seventy-five other military personnel. We arrived at Kai Tak International Airport in Hong Kong three hours later and were bussed to the hotel. I undressed, laid the belts out on the bed, and took a shower. I then called the number that Lalchand had given me and a very professional voice announced that he would be right over. In less than fifteen minutes, there was a knock on the door.

I opened the door and four men entered the room. One was very slim and businesslike; the other three were "goons" right out of the movies. The businessman stuck out his hand and introduced himself. He was Lalchand's cousin. The others didn't say a word. As soon as they spotted the belts on the bed, they unzipped the pockets and dumped the cash out into a pile. The cousin took me aside, led me over to the window overlooking Kowloon harbor, and began to make small talk and point out some of the local sites. I could hear the rustling of money being counted behind me. I was very, very nervous. Suppose Lalchand had miscounted the money when he loaded up the belts? Would my headless body be found floating face down in the harbor?

After several minutes I heard someone say, "It's OK." The cousin smiled broadly. Immediately the tension in the room dissolved and even the solemn goons were smiling. Lalchand's cousin went over to the bed and picked up one of the piles of $100 bills. He meticulously counted off twenty-five bills and handed them to me.

"Good job," he said. "Now, let's enjoy Hong Kong. The rest of the week is on me. Let's go eat!"

I tried to demur, but he was very insistent. The henchmen stuffed all of the money into several briefcases that they had brought with them and we took the elevator down to the lobby. The cousin and I turned right and the others turned left as we exited the hotel.

The week in Hong Kong was a true Bacchanalian festival. I was wined, dined, and taken care of for five glorious days. To my amazement each morning a different lady showed up at my room to be my personal Hong Kong guide. Each was more beautiful than the previous and they all spoke educated English with a British lilt. They took me to the best restaurants and catered to my every need. The cousin apparently had access to a large stable of Eurasian beauties and I felt that I had died and gone to heaven. By Friday, I was exhausted and looking forward to getting back to Saigon. Best of all, I was going home with an extra $2,500 in my pocket.

Six months later I was able to finagle another R & R to Hong Kong. This time Lalchand had figured out how to send me with $100,000. The entire trip was a carbon copy of the previous one, but the commission was an impressive $5,000. About a year later, I had an opportunity to go to Penang on R & R. The word on the street, however, was that the military and the FBI had a large number of undercover operatives trying to gather information on black market currency exchangers. I got cold feet and decided not to press my luck. This soldier did not want to be the first GI hung publicly for currency manipulation. I stayed away from Lalchand's store for a number of weeks.

Several years later I ran into an old friend from Vietnam at a wedding in Falls Church, Virginia. He told me that Lalchand had been caught red-handed by the Vietnamese authorities, tried, convicted, and sentenced to death. About a month after his arrest, the sentence was publicly carried out by firing squad to impress the populace with the severity of his crime.

Chapter 21
Ongoing

Random Ramblings

Visits to the Zoo

When I had time on my hands, I often visited the Saigon Zoological Gardens. This peaceful corner of Saigon, with its winding paths and cages of pacing animals, provided an opportunity to sit and contemplate the world. Although the zoo was never crowded on any given day, visiting families, excited children in tow, filed throughout the gardens to pass the time caught up in an exciting natural world.

I loved to wander among the animals, my two favorites being the chimpanzee and the Philippine monkey-eating eagle. The chimpanzee got to know me on sight because I always handed him a cigarette or two to chew. Even if I offered him a lit cigarette, this intelligent critter would snuff it out on the floor of his cage and then eat it. A sign on the railing in front of his cage warned people not to feed the chimpanzee. I usually ignored this warning and every time I approached the cage, kids would appear out of nowhere to see what was going to happen. This chimp was so conditioned to my presence, that as soon as he saw me, he would begin to chatter and sit with his back against the bars. This was my cue to deliver a vigorous back scratching. In return for the privilege, he expected a cigarette.

One day, as he turned around to take a cigarette from my hand, he reached through the bars and grabbed the front of my shirt. As I recoiled, he ripped the entire front of my shirt off, buttons and all. He retreated to the middle of his cage where he proceeded to put the piece of cloth on his head, in his mouth, and over his shoulder. He paraded around in the cage to show everyone what he had. I was livid but totally helpless to retaliate. The spectators laughed uproariously at the chimpanzee's antics.

At this moment, one of the zoo keepers arrived and proceeded to berate me for stepping over the railing. I had no comeback. He told me that a recurrence of this event would result in me being permanently banned from the park. I apologized profusely and the keeper turned and left. Suddenly it dawned on me that the spectators were not laughing at the chimp but were laughing at my stupidity. I stood in the middle of the park, an embarrassed jerk wearing 2/3 of a shirt.

The Philippine monkey-eating eagle was one of the most impressive birds that I had even seen. His cage was 25–30 feet high and about 150–200 feet around. Most of the time the eagle sat majestically on his high perch at the top of his cage. He stood about 4½ feet tall, and had a wingspread of over eight feet (according to the sign attached to the cage). I have seen pictures of giant condors, but this eagle seemed to be equivalent in size. Its alert beady eyes constantly scanned the ground for anything that moved.

Every two or three days, the eagle was fed by releasing several live squirrel monkeys into the cage. When the eagle was ready, he would swoop down and nail his first course. I saw this gruesome spectacle only once and made a point thereafter to visit only on non-feeding days. One time when I went to see the eagle, the keeper happened to be in the cage doing routine cleaning with a hose. Apparently the eagle thought that the hose was a large black snake and swooped down to grab it. Water shot everywhere: on the keeper, on the spectators, and on me. I got soaked to the skin! Everyone thought that it was hilariously funny that the American got wet, yet all I could sputter was the Vietnamese equivalent of "Shit Happens!"

Let's Pay a Visit

During my two tours of duty in Vietnam, I drew monthly combat pay just like all of the other military personnel in country. The only requirement to receive a month's combat pay was to spend four hours of any day in that month in the combat zone. Enlisted men were paid $75 and officers were paid $125. In addition, a soldier's pay and allowances were tax exempt if earned in a combat zone. What a license to steal—and steal, they did! On the last day of every month, one could go over to the passenger terminal at Tan Son Nhut and watch the military planes coming in one right after the other. Their precious cargo? Officers coming from all over the Far East to conduct "inspection tours" of military installations in Vietnam.

Each of the services was represented. All the officer had to do was be in country during the last four hours of the last day of the month and the first four hours of the next day. This garnered them two months worth of combat pay and tax exemptions! A cool $250 could be had for just showing up! I once estimated that over two hundred officers came to visit on the last day of every month. Many officers brought enlisted members from their staff so they could also "slop at the trough" of combat pay.

I was also aware that many of the inspection tours were conducted from hotel rooms and brothels. Guys like me had to literally make reservations at our favorite cathouse whenever the end of the month rolled around. I knew one Major stationed in Japan who would fly in at around 7:30 P.M. on the last day of the month, spend the night eating, drinking, and whoring and then fly back around 6:00 A.M. the next day. His wife and kids back in Japan were never the wiser.

All I Want to Do is Die

My joint interrogation team had been working in the area of Loc Ninh, a district town about eight miles from the Cambodian border and almost sixty miles north of Saigon. One evening three of us went into town to check it out. As we were walking along one of the streets, the sweet smell of tobacco attracted me to one of the shops. I stuck my head in the door and immediately realized that I was looking into an opium den. I pushed aside a beaded curtain and, in the dimly lit room, I could make out six elderly men sitting cross-legged on the floor. Each of the men was seated in front of a Maxwell House coffee can filled with dirt and containing a 3–4" round clay bowl from which a pipe stem emanated. I was ready to turn around and continue my walk when a sleek middle-aged woman approached me.

"You want to try?" she asked. I looked at my two buddies. They nodded affirmatively. I nodded to the woman that we wanted to try. She quickly produced three more coffee can contraptions for smoking opium. I didn't think twice since I was currently smoking almost two packs a day of unfiltered Pall Mall cigarettes. I sat on the floor and the woman placed a thimble-sized gummy ball of something in the bowl of my pipe. She lit the wad and turned the can toward me so that I could use the pipe stem. I figured that I would take one or two puffs, get a little high, and enjoy a wonderful evening on the town. I took a deep inhale of the smoke. The reaction took about ten seconds. I felt like I had just hit a brick wall while going 60 miles an hour on a bicycle. My eyeballs began to ache, I began coughing uncontrollably, and I could not stand up. I kept gasping for air. My two friends were experiencing exactly the same sensations. Someone or something then figuratively hit me in the head with a twenty-pound sledge hammer. I tried to get up. It was futile. I crawled toward the door and rolled out onto the sidewalk. I lay there for what seemed like hours. Two Vietnamese teenagers tried to help me get up. I was finally able to sit up straight on the curb. My head was pounding like I was inside the bell tower at Westminster Abbey. I had a major case of the "dry heaves." I couldn't stop heaving and I kept gagging on my own spittle.

After about two hours I tried to drink a cup of hot tea. I threw it up immediately. For the next six days I tried to eat something every day. It was impossible. Even chicken soup was out of the question. I have never been so ill in my life previously or since. All I wanted to do was die peacefully in my sleep. Let's just say that opium and Pete Fournier is a match made in hell!

Howard Johnson

If one walked out of the front gate of Davis Station, made a right, and walked about 300 yards down the dirt road, one would come upon a neatly constructed cement block ranch house with an attached carport. Inside the carport were six picnic tables with benches and a large charcoal grill. Hanging from the front of the carport was a hand-lettered sign indicating that this was "Howard Johnson", a local restaurant. If you didn't notice the sign you could still tell that this was a Howard Johnson from the bright orange roof. The word was that there had been an Army engineer company nearby and that this company had several 5-gallon buckets of metal primer in their warehouse with no immediate purpose for it. One of the guys was wondering how to get rid of it when someone suggested that the local snack bar could be christened "Howard Johnson" and the roof could be painted with the orange paint. It was easy to convince the proprietor who was an ARVN soldier by day and a restaurateur by night. He would get a free paint job for his carport. Also, the ARVN soldier kind of liked the name and encouraged the clientele to call him "Howard". The menu that Howard and his wife had put together included grilled chicken, grilled beef (really water buffalo), grilled pork, grilled fish, and grilled dog. Any of the entrees were available with a side of grilled sweet potato or grilled squash and a small bowl of white rice. A soft drink was included, but an Export 33 was about 50¢ extra. A complete meal could be had for about 75 piasters (99¢). Most of my friends and I had no qualms about eating at Howard Johnson because everything was overcooked.

Many days Howard would not report for duty with his unit. He was making more money in the restaurant business than as a soldier. His commanding officer didn't seem to much care who showed up and who didn't as long as his palm was adequately greased by the no-shows. The general officer in Howard's chain of command had purchased his command for about $20,000 from General Thieu, one of his old school classmates.

One day in January I was sitting around shooting the bull with Howard when I noticed a large cage sitting in the sun at the back of the carport. There appeared to be a reptile of some kind inside the cage. I walked over to the cage and Howard followed me.

"What is this?" I asked Howard.

"An anaconda" he replied. (I looked up the word later in my Vietnamese–English dictionary.)

"Wow, it's very large," I commented.

"Yes, about four meters," he replied. "I'm fattening it up for Tet."

"For Tet?" A puzzled expression crept across my face.

"Yeah, my wife and I are having our families over and I wanted to serve something special."

I screwed up my nose in disbelief.

"What the hell does it taste like?" I inquired. "Con trăn ăn giống như thịt gà (Boa constrictor tastes just like chicken!)," he replied.

Four for You, One for Me

I was walking to my favorite bar along a street that overlooked the main Saigon docks. An American cargo ship had docked and was being unloaded by American stevedores and Vietnamese laborers. I stopped to watch all of the activity below me. Forklifts, dollies, and cranes were moving back and forth in a frenzy. It looked like ants swarming over a large anthill. My attention was drawn to several US Army 2½-ton trucks parked near one of the unloading ramps. American stevedores were loading the trucks with refrigerators stacked on palettes. I also noticed a large flatbed Volvo truck parked in the area that had Vietnamese markings on it. A Vietnamese man was operating a forklift and putting palettes of refrigerators onto the flatbed. The ratio seemed to be one palette onto the flatbed for every four palettes loaded into the Army trucks. I wondered what was going on. I stood and watched for about twenty minutes. The instant that the Volvo truck seemed fully loaded, a Vietnamese driver appeared and drove it away. I had also noticed a well-dressed Vietnamese man who had been coordinating the entire loading process. As soon as the truck was gone, he seemed to be negotiating something with another man, an American. Their arms were flailing wildly and the conversation seemed to be very heated. Finally, the Vietnamese man took a wad of money out of his pocket and peeled off a number of bills, most of which he gave to the American. At this moment, a Mercedes limousine pulled up and the Vietnamese man got into the back seat. The limousine sped away.

When I arrived at the bar, I told the mamasan about what I had observed. She smiled wryly and informed me that I had seen "Mr. Big" of the Vietnamese black market. He literally controlled the Saigon docks and bought what he wanted and at the price of his choosing. Anyone who got in his way was generally eliminated. I just sat there dumbfounded.

I was jolted out of my daze when the mamasan announced, "He's really a nice guy. As a matter of fact, he's my favorite brother-in-law."

Shopping Tips

Two of the thorniest problems while shopping were:

1.   How to deal with shoe shine boys, and

2.   How to tell ivory from plastic.

When you walked along the streets of Saigon, Hue, Da Nang, or any other city, the sidewalks seemed to be controlled by shoe shine boys. About every 100 feet there was a kid or two, armed with shoe polish, shoe brushes, and rags waiting to pounce on you to convince you that you needed your shoes or boots shined. Even if they noticed that you had just had it done down the street, they wanted to convince you that you needed a "reshine." If you were walking at a certain pace and you slowed down, even imperceptibly, they took this as a sign that you wanted your shoes shined. They would intercept you on the sidewalk and, while one kid tried to distract you, the other kid was already on his knees applying polish. Before you could compose yourself, you had one shoe with unbuffed polish on it and one shoe with no polish on it. What could you do? You couldn't keep going with two unlike shoes! I can even recall one especially aggressive kid who had perfected the art of shining shoes while the customer was still moving. Well, it didn't take me long to buy a pair of PF Keds sneakers to wear when I went downtown. Or, now and then I would wear sandals. One day I stopped a boy, took off my sandals, and told him that I needed my feet polished. He didn't know what to do! Score one for the good guys!

The other fun thing to do was shop for objects made from ivory. I would stop at a vendor's stall and begin to admire a statue or something allegedly made from ivory. I really had a hard time differentiating between the two. My friend Lalchand told me how to tell the difference. I would ask the vendor if the object I was looking at was made out of ivory. I was always assured that it was.

"Finest elephant ivory," was the mantra.

"Then you shouldn't worry if I test the ivory," I would reply.

At this point I would take my Zippo lighter from my pocket and begin to heat the object. If the object was made from ivory, only soot from the flame would be deposited. This rubbed off easily with a handkerchief. If the object was plastic, it would start to melt and liquefy. I can't explain the look on a merchant's face when you have caught him (or her) red-handed in a lie. They just stand there dumbstruck!

Not "Unforgettable"

The USO shows appeared monthly at both the NCO Club and the Officer's Club at the 175th RRC. On show nights draft beers were 10¢ and shots of liquor were 25¢. Thus, one could do a shot-and-a-beer for the princely sum of 35¢. I was usually feeling no pain after two of these. The shows generally consisted of two Australian singers accompanied by two musicians, one with a guitar and one with a saxophone. The repertoire was usually American classic songs or Top 40. However, one thing was a constant. During one of the sets, you could count on hearing "Danny Boy" and, during one of the other sets, you could count on hearing "I Left My Heart in San Francisco." Sometimes, the singers would even perform them back-to-back. I heard those two goddamn songs so many times I wanted to scream. No matter where I went in Vietnam, a USO show at a club would always include them. Even today, if I begin to hear one of them, I immediately turn off the radio or mute the TV. I can "Name That Tune" in two notes.

Chapter 22
October 1967

O, Canada!

One morning, Lalchand and I were sitting around shooting the bull when he came up with a suggestion that really made me sit up and take notice. Would I like to go to Vung Tau with him and his live-in?

"I'd like nothing better," I replied enthusiastically.

Vung Tau was a resort city located about seventy-five miles east of Saigon on Highway One. The French had named the city Cap St. Jacques, and the well-to-do of Europe vacationed there in the 1920s and 1930s. The city was always noted for its ability to "look the other way" toward debauchery and immorality. At the time, prostitution was legal and women were supposed to carry a yellow 3 x 5 card to show that the local health department had declared them free of venereal disease.

The city was also noted for an active twenty-four-hour "Business District" where one could be pursued by young boys selling packs of *Kool* cigarettes. These filtered cigarettes had been opened and the tobacco skillfully replaced with pot so that only a seasoned expert could detect any tampering. Furthermore, these same young boys might ask if you wanted to "boom boom" their sister because "She number one cherry girl. She virgin."

The next day Lalchand arrived at 8:00 A.M. sharp. I immediately noticed that he was alone and when I asked him where his girlfriend was he told me that she had had a death in the family and would not be coming with us.

"OK," I said as I jumped into Lalchand's 1959 Renault, lit up a cigarette, and settled back in the seat.

We headed east down Highway One toward our destination and had gone about ten miles when I noticed that I had forgotten my wallet and my money back in the officer quarters.

"Don't worry about a thing," Lalchand assured me when I told him of my predicament. I'll take care of everything and you can repay me when we got back."

That sounded OK to me, so I lit up again and relaxed.

We were traveling at about forty miles per hour and passing the usual complement of oxcarts, bicycles, mopeds, and pedestrians when I began to notice that people along the side of the road were waving frantically and pointing in the direction in which we were traveling. Suddenly, I broke into a cold sweat. I had completely forgotten! The previous week I had seen an announcement putting this stretch of Highway One off limits to casual Americans. Only convoys and armored vehicles were allowed in the area. When I told Lalchand what I had read, he laughed.

"Take it easy, Peter. I know my way around this country like the back of my hand. No worries as long as you're with me." He stared straight ahead and stepped on the gas.

"But I really think we should turn around and head back to Saigon," I cautioned. "This is not something I think we should be dealing with."

My experience with Intelligence made me wary and ill at ease.

Lalchand turned a deaf ear to my concern, so I eventually held my peace and let him speed ahead. Minutes later we rounded a bend in the road where up ahead we could see traffic slowing down to a halt. *An accident?* I wondered. I craned my neck and, in the distance, I could make out that cars were being stopped at some kind of a checkpoint. *Curious*, I thought. *This is a high-speed road. Why would there be a checkpoint?* Some of the cars ahead of us were being waved through. As we got within about fifty feet of the checkpoint I could see uniformed personnel with rifles peering into the back seats and trunks of the stopped vehicles. My mind raced to put the picture together. And then it hit me: these were Viet Cong soldiers!

"Oh! Shit!" I barked at Lalchand. "Those are VC!" He turned white.

"Let me do the talking," he directed as a young soldier approached, pointed his AK-47 rifle into the car, and asked Lalchand where he was going. "To Vung Tau on business," Lalchand told him smoothly.

The soldier asked Lalchand his name and then turned his attention to me.

"What is your nationality?" the soldier demanded. "Tôi là người Xa-na-da (I am Canadian)," I responded.

At this point every hair bristled on the back of my neck, but I struggled to maintain calm.

"I don't believe you," he retorted. "You are one of the American pigs!"

His angry eyes darted from me, to Lalchand, to the backseat of the car, and back again to me.

"No. No. Xa-na-da!" I insisted.

Now sweat began to pour down the center of my back. It was all I could do to maintain my outward composure.

"Get out of the car!" the soldier ordered.

I turned to slide out when another soldier approached. He grabbed my arm and yanked me to a standing position.

"What are you doing here?" he demanded. Lalchand intervened.

"We are members of the "Ủy-hội Kiêm-soát Quốc-tế (International Control Commission[1])," Lalchand declared. "If you harm us, you will have the international community to deal with."

The two soldiers laughed. I was utterly taken aback by Lalchand's quick thinking. This was perfect! He would claim that he was from India and I would insist that I was from Canada. Problem solved! But this solution was but a pipe dream! Lalchand and I were ordered to put our hands behind our backs where they were securely bound. We were then marched into the dense undergrowth by the side of the road. The soldiers seemed to enjoy using the butt end of their rifles as human cattle prods and they kept hitting us in the center of our knees and backs to make us march faster. After we had gone about a

---

1.　The International Control Commission was an arm of the United Nations which had been sent to Vietnam in 1954 to oversee the orderly emigration of people from the North to the South. The three member nations of the Commission were Canada, India, and Poland.

hundred yards into the forest, we came to what looked like a Viet Cong encampment. Congregating there were fifty or sixty soldiers who swarmed at our approach and began to beat us unmercifully in the head, arms, legs, and crotch. I felt my left arm snap like a piece of kindling. Blood streamed down my face and I gagged on the bile that rose from the pit of my stomach. Kicking and screaming I was dragged across the camp and thrown into a bamboo cage just large enough to allow me to sit with my knees bent. I passed out several times, then came to, aware of the overpowering stench of my own feces. The VC bastards had literally "beaten the shit out of me." I fainted again.

I awoke face down in the mud. Turning slightly I looked up into the face of a Viet Cong officer standing over me, a dark monument to evil silhouetted against the impending night.

"Get up!" he screamed and slammed his foot into my ribs.

Barely managing to stand, I propped myself against a nearby palm tree. Two soldiers grabbed me and dragged me into a makeshift tent. There I was ordered to sit down at a small wooden table.

Suddenly the tent opening darkened and was filled with the menacing figure of the VC officer.

"I am Major Phuc," he announced sharply. "And who are you?"

"Pete Fournier," I managed to spit out.

"I have to take your word for it because you have no identification. How do I know that you are a Canadian?"

"You'll have to take my word for it," I countered.

"I don't take anybody's word for anything!" he screamed in my face.

Obviously angered, he walked around the table several times, all the while pinning me to my seat with his eyes. Through my bloody haze I could see the wheels turning in his mind. Abruptly he stuck his ugly nose two inches from my face.

"Listen, you lying American son-of-a-bitch!

His breath, a combination of putrid fish and *nước mắm,*[2] sent my stomach reeling.

I suddenly heard Lalchand yelling for help. They were working him over pretty well.

I shouted back, "Hang on, Guy. We should both be dead in a few minutes!"

The Major slapped me across the mouth—and then dropped a verbal atom bomb.

"Alright, mother fucker. Five years ago I was a student at the University of Montreal. If you're a Canadian, you should know your own national anthem. START SINGING!"

On cue, I began to mumble the words to the Canadian national anthem in French[3]:

---

2.   The national fish sauce of Vietnam, eaten with or used in preparing many seafood dishes.

3.   My father was born in Quebec province of Canada and emigrated to the U.S. when he was a teenager. My mother was born in a French Canadian neighborhood in Lynn, Massachusetts. When I was growing up with four siblings in New Jersey, we spoke only French at home. We were taught the Canadian national anthem in French and we used to sing it along with other French songs.

Ô Canada!
Terre de nos aïeux,
Ton front est ceint de fleurons glorieux!
Car ton bras sait porter l'épée,
Il sait porter la croix!
Ton histoire. . .

The Major's eyes changed from slanted to round. He could not believe what he was hearing.

"OK. Stop, Stop," he said as he waved his arms wildly.

I could see a look of embarrassment spreading over his face. He began to speak softly and with compassion.

"Messieur Fournier, I'm so sorry!"

He motioned to one of his men standing nearby.

"Take him away."

A Viet Cong soldier helped me to my feet, supporting me as we left the tent. Two other soldiers joined us and they carefully carried me back out to Highway One. There they gently put me down on the shoulder of the road and disappeared back into the bush. Several minutes later, Lalchand was dumped next to me. He looked the worst for wear, but somehow we had both managed to survive a trip through a virtual whirring sausage machine!

Slowly I got up and tried to walk. I managed two full steps before I fell. I could see Lalchand's car parked on the shoulder about fifty yards away. Between walking and crawling, we were both able to finally make it to the car. I looked at my reflection in the front window. My face looked like I had just gone fifteen rounds with Rocky Marciano and he had landed 100% of his punches. I lay down on the back seat and Lalchand propped himself up in the front seat. We both passed out.

When I awoke, there were three American soldiers peering at us from outside the car.

They asked the obvious, "What the fuck happened to you guys?"

"We've had a little accident," Lalchand quickly responded.

One of the soldiers looked puzzled.

"So where's the damage to the car?"

"It doesn't matter, Soldier," Lalchand replied. "Just get us to a hospital. I'm Indian and he's Canadian, and we both need help. Right now!"

We were escorted to a jeep. One of the soldiers got behind the wheel of the Renault and we all took off toward Saigon. I must have passed out several more times. When I finally came to my senses, I was in a hospital bed hooked up to several IVs.

The next morning a member of the International Red Cross came to visit me. I told him my whole story.

All he could say was, "Lieutenant, you're one lucky bastard."

I truly realized that two insignificant events had saved my life: knowing the Canadian national anthem in French and accidentally leaving my wallet on the bunk.

I had asked the Red Cross volunteer to contact my commanding officer at the 175th RRC, and the next day he came to visit. I told him about the terrible automobile accident I had been in while riding in a taxicab in Saigon. The Captain swallowed my story hook, line, and sinker. If the truth had been known, I would have been court-martialed for violating an off-limits declaration. Instead, the Captain sympathized with my plight and sent other soldiers from the unit to visit me during the week that I was in the hospital. When I returned to the unit, I was treated with compassion and respect by everyone, and I was even excused from filling sandbags to put around the officer quarters. I had really dodged a bullet—and all due to the Canadian National anthem!

Chapter 23
December 1967

Tea for Twenty Two

All of the bars in Viet Nam operated on the "Saigon Tea" system. Let's say an American came in, sat at the bar, and ordered a beer. He would be immediately approached by one of the bar girls. The conversation would generally be as follows:

"Hi, my name Loan. What your name?"

"I'm Bill."

"Hi Bill. You buy me Saigon tea?"

Bill's answer depended on whether or not he wanted female companionship. If Bill said "No," he would be told that he was "number 100" and the bar girl would wander away.

If Bill said "Yes," the bar girl would signal to the barmaid to bring over a glass of tea. It wasn't really a glass; it was more like a clear plastic thimble filled with weak Chinese tea. The cost of a "Saigon Tea" was about 100 piasters ($1.30 US). When the tea arrived, Bill's new companion would propose a toast.

"Chin, chin, Ho Chi Minh," was the favorite.

The tea was quickly downed and a request for another tea followed immediately. Of course, the bar girl was now kissing Bill on the cheek and maybe even had her hand on his thigh. How could Bill resist? Another tea arrived. Within a matter of twenty minutes, Bill could easily purchase anywhere from ten to fifteen teas. The more teas that Bill bought, the more attention he got. If business was slow, one or two other bar girls may have joined in and were now rubbing Bill's back or kissing him. It was an easy jump to Bill buying teas three at a time. The instant that Bill had drained his beer, another one appeared on the bar. The objective was to get Bill just drunk enough that he would offer no resistance to multiple tea purchases.

The bar girls were getting 33% of the proceeds from the tea that they pushed. The barmaid kept a tally by name on a sheet of paper near the cash register. The girls were paid every day at the end of their shift. An aggressive bar girl could easily make $30 per day just on tea sales.

The other major source of revenue for bar girls was sex. There were two varieties, "short time" and "all night." A "short time" lasted about fifteen minutes and excluded almost all foreplay. The cost was about 500 piasters ($6.50 US). The split with the mamasan was generally 50-50. On the other hand, an "all night" session lasted about forty-five minutes. Here nothing was off limits and the bar girl would do just about anything you wanted. The cost of an "all night" was about 1000 piasters ($13.00 US). What a deal!

On occasion, the girl required use of a condom. Since most GIs didn't carry their own, they had to pay an extra 200 piasters for a house-supplied condom. The four or five service rooms were usually located at the back of the bar building and most had doors that could be closed and locked from the inside. Each room was equipped with a single military cot, a three-foot high earthenware vase filled with water, and a supply of small towels. Both parties would clean up with soap and water ladled from the earthenware vase.

One hot, lazy weekday afternoon in Saigon I settled into a booth at *The International Bar* to enjoy a lunch of noodles with beef. There were only six or so customers in the bar and the eight unoccupied bar girls were chattering, laughing, and gossiping. The front door was wide open to allow any semblance of a breeze to waft through the bar, and all of the ceiling fans were set at medium speed. I noticed a tall individual come into the bar. He looked around for a moment and then sat down into one of the easy chairs that were set up near the front of the bar. One of the idle bar girls came over and asked him what he wanted. He ordered a Budweiser and asked for a menu. She told him that they could call out for anything that he wanted.

"You want cheeseburger?" she asked. He nodded yes.

"Lettuce, tomato, onion?" Again, he nodded yes.

The bar girl motioned to a young boy who was hanging around and told him to go get the food. About fifteen minutes later the boy returned with a brown paper bag. The customer ate ravenously.

While the boy was gone, two of the other bar girls started to "work the customer." Four Saigon teas had already been ordered. From where I was sitting I could see and hear everything that was going on. The guy's name was Harold, he was from California, and he was a civilian employee of the Merchant Marine. He had just arrived in

Saigon after being at sea for six weeks. When he paid for his first beer and cheeseburger, he pulled out a thick wad of MPCs that had not yet been converted into piasters.

When the mamasan came over and explained that they did not accept MPCs, I entered the conversation and told Harold that he would have to go around the corner to the Bank of America and convert his money into local currency. I told him to give me a 20-spot to pay his bill and to come back later. Harold got up and left.

About thirty minutes later Harold reappeared. He sat down and ordered another beer and I asked him if the exchange had worked out OK. He replied that he now had twice as many bills in his pocket as before. I could see wads of money in both of his pants pockets and both of his shirt pockets. Harold was ready to party!

This time three girls started working on Harold. One sat on his lap and one sat on each arm of the chair. They began to order Saigon tea two at a time. When the barmaid came over to collect, Harold just took three bills and handed them to her. When she came with change, Harold just motioned for her to keep it. As soon as Harold would finish a can of Budweiser, another one would appear. Saigon tea was now arriving six and eight at a time. Whenever Harold would look away, the girls would dump tea behind his chair or into the base of the palm tree nearby. After an hour, Harold began to feel the beer. His speech became slurred and he ordered Saigon teas by the dozen. I estimated that he had put away about six beers and had ordered over fifty Saigon teas. Periodically, one of the girls would rub Harold's crotch. Harold reveled in the attention. I guess that six weeks at sea had taken its toll.

Eventually, Harold dozed off. When he awoke, the girls started working him over again. This time he was drinking Coca Cola, but he was still buying Saigon teas by the dozen. Harold was being taken for everything he had.

Harold now decided that he wanted something extra for his money. He inquired about the price of a little fellatio. One of the girls told him 500 piasters. Harold looked over at me for approval.

I shook my head "No" and said, "Too much."

Harold countered with an offer of 250. His offer was accepted and the girl that had been sitting on his lap proceeded to "do her thing." One of the other girls lifted her miniskirt and began to "moon" Harold. I would have given a thousand dollars to have had a camera at this point. Five other girls came over to cheer on the two "performers." It was obvious that Harold was in another world as he was audibly purring and orchestrating the earthy activities of the two girls. Could it be that we were all characters in a Federico Fellini film?

After several minutes I grew quite bored with the proceedings. I paid my bill and left. I wandered around the central market, did some window shopping, checked out what was new at the sidewalk black markets, and stopped in to see my Pakistani friend, Lalchand. Later, I decided to stop back at *The International Bar* to see how Harold was doing. I walked in and sat down in the same booth. Harold was quite inebriated. Additionally, he was now buying Saigon tea by the tray. A tray held about 25 teas. Harold would just hand the barmaid a bunch of piaster notes and tell her to take what she needed to cover the bill. I was disgusted that this guy was being taken for everything that he was worth. On the other hand, I felt that he was a grown man and he should know better! I got up to leave.

On the way out, I shook Harold's hand and said "I hope everything turns out OK, buddy".

He mumbled something about "See ya in the weeds."

I couldn't stop thinking about poor Harold. So, several days later, I stopped in at *The International Bar* and sought out the mamasan. I asked her if Harold made it through the day OK. She said that he finally left at about 10 P.M. and whispered that he had spent 500,000 piasters.

"500,000 piasters?" I repeated the number twice in Vietnamese. She nodded that I was correct.

In my mind I did some quick arithmetic. "Let's see, at 77 piasters to the dollar. . . ." The mamasan eyed me patiently while I toyed with the calculations.

"Holy shit! That's 6,500 dollars!" I couldn't believe what I had just said. In nine hours, this guy had spent $6,500! That's $722 per hour! I said to the mamasan, "I hope he had a good time!"

She smiled at me with knowing eyes and replied in broken English, "He say he come back next month. He dinky dow (crazy), for sure!"

I laughed and said, "For Sure!"

Chapter 24
January 1968

Creative Business Ideas

One of my mamasan friends was a wealthy entrepreneur. She owned three bars and two steam baths in Saigon. One of her bars, *The International Palace*, was her base of operations. She and I would sit by the hour sipping "Ba Muoi Ba" (Export 33) and discussing her various businesses. Like any business owner, most of her problems were labor-related, and she was concerned with the constant turnover of her employees.

"How to hire and retain good employees, Mr. Phong. No find good employees any more," she would bitterly complain.

I found this very amusing because she was referring to prostitutes and other sex workers.

One day the mamasan was bemoaning the fact that business was extremely slow from about 1:00 P.M. to 5:00 P.M. seven days a week. Since the steam baths opened at noon, and business really didn't start to come in until early evening, they had several unproductive hours.

"What to do with all this idle time, Mr. Phong?" The mamasan was actually quite concerned that her business was less efficient than it could be. I sat back and considered. The usual charge for a steam bath, a massage, and a blowjob was about 400 piasters (about $5.00 US). And then it hit me!

"Mamasan, why don't you drop the price to 200 piasters from 1:00 to 5:00 P.M. and call it 'The Blue Plate Special'? You could put signs in the windows during those hours and I guarantee they will attract a lot more walk-in traffic. Most Americans are familiar with the term 'Blue Plate Special.' They'll find it amusing."

I wrote "Ask Us About Our Blue Plate Special" on a napkin for her. She said that she would have several signs made and, sure enough, the following week the signs appeared in the front windows of both of her steam baths.

The sex workers at the steam baths were a comical bunch. They tended to be old peasant women in their 60s who wore classic black pajamas and conical hats. Their few remaining teeth were stained black from chewing betel nut. From a strictly aesthetic point of view, they were probably the homeliest women that you could imagine. Most guys kept their eyes shut during the fellatio phase of the visit. The oral sex was not mandatory.

After the massage phase was completed, the attendant usually asked, "You want suckee?"

According to the mamasan, about half of the customers opted out.

The revenue generated from these activities was split 1/3 to the employee, 2/3 to the owner. Each worker received two days off per week, and one week of paid vacation each year. (The amount paid was based on historical revenue data kept by the mamasan). The workers arranged their schedule amongst themselves. Each establishment had a receptionist/cashier to generally oversee the day-to-day operations. These women were also expected to fill in as needed if business was overly brisk or if one of the other workers "called in sick." The entire operation ran like clockwork, thanks to the good management practices of the women.

A good sex worker could earn more in one day than a Major in the South Vietnamese Army could earn in a week. The mamasan of *The International Palace* was grossing about five times what her Colonel husband was earning. Her largest expense after commissions, however, lay in the "licensing fees" that had to be paid to the Saigon Chief of Police, the Head of the Licensing Bureau, the Mayor of Saigon, and various other local government functionaries. She even had to pay protection money to several gangs of neighborhood thugs simply to ensure that no "accidental" fires were set. Overall, the mamasan was able to net about 25% of the gross. This amounted to about $10,000 US dollars per month. She once offered to pay me $1,000 per month in consulting fees. I declined her offer but did take her up on her offer of "freebies" from her stable of bar girls.

Another sex business that was prominent in Saigon and throughout Vietnam was the "masturbation palace." This consisted of a room in a commercial building where about fifteen hospital gurneys were set up in three rows of five gurneys. Each gurney was "manned" by one worker. Associated with each gurney was a small table on which was placed a family size jar of Vaseline and a box of Kleenex. The customer would lay half-naked and face up on the gurney. The cost was about 300 piasters ($3.90 US) payable in advance.

The atmosphere in the room was truly surreal. There were always a number of customers who were groaning in ecstasy. But the interesting part was to observe the workers. As they stroked away, they would nonchalantly chat among themselves about family, friends, boyfriends, problems in school, etc. There was little or no conversation between the worker and the customer. The women were taking gossip to a new level. They would also compare "joints" by making jokes about length, girth, and lack of straightness. They would talk negatively about the ugly Americans who patronized their establishment. The workers seemed totally detached from what they were doing. The atmosphere could have easily been mistaken for a class reunion of the all-girls Saigon Academic Institute for Women. Some of the workers were putting themselves through college or helping a sibling pay tuition. Others were paying room and board at home because their parents were very poor. Oral sex and intercourse were strictly forbidden. If the subject even came up, the standard indignant response was, "What do you think I am? A whore?" Surprisingly, most of the workers were well dressed and well groomed.

The only time that I patronized one of these establishments was during my first week in Vietnam. A friend of mine who had been in country for six months briefed me on what goes on inside. I decided to check out the one that he recommended. What followed was one of the most culturally interesting incidents during my two-year stay in Vietnam. Before I entered the establishment I decided that I would "play dumb," and not let the workers know that I spoke and understood Vietnamese. I paid the admission charge and picked out a gurney manned by the most attractive worker in the room. I stretched out on the gurney and nodded that I was ready for her to begin. She immediately began to make disparaging remarks to her co-workers about my anatomy. She also verbalized her hatred of Americans and all things American. She seemed to be a Viet Cong sympathizer. I bit my tongue and waited for the session to end. During the entire session she had never cracked even a hint of a smile. I had become quite angry but I was able to temporarily suppress my anger.

I slid off the gurney and pulled up my pants. I then dropped the mother of all bombs.

I turned to the girl and said, in perfect Vietnamese, "Your technique could use some work. And so could your tongue, bitch."

She turned whiter than the whitest sheet and began to tremble. *How much of her conversation had the American understood?*

"For two cents I'd shove that Vaseline jar down your goddamn throat," I roared. "You are the lowest scum I have ever known."

All of the activity in the room came to an abrupt halt. I was sure that the girl was going to pass out. She screamed and ran out of the room. Five of the other girls followed immediately behind, sheer terror etched across their faces. I could hear the front door being pulled open and then slammed shut behind them.

The remaining girls let out a collective sigh of relief. One of them came over to me.

"We all hated Hong," she confided. "If she never comes back, it will be too soon."

Someone had finally stood up to the dominating and intimidating Hong and suddenly I was the hero of the moment.

I found out later from my mamasan friend that Hong, in fact, was a Viet Cong spy. Unbeknownst to anyone, she had been planted in the establishment to find out where and when American soldiers thought the next battles would be and what Americans knew about the location of Viet Cong units around the capital. I also found out that she never returned to work after that night.

Several weeks later I ran into the girl who had congratulated me. She was doing her food shopping in the central market. She asked me my name and I told her that it was Ong Phong. She told me that her name was Phung. She invited me to her home for dinner with her family. I readily accepted and Phung gave me a date, time, and address. She also asked me where I had learned to speak "earthy" Vietnamese. I told her that I had studied Vietnamese at an American university and that in the process I had picked up many useful terms. Phung still couldn't believe what she had experienced that evening.

Phung also told me that her dream was to work for the US Embassy. I asked her about her English language skills but she admitted that they were very weak. I suggested that she look into attending *The British School* on Hai Ba Trung Street. She said that her sister had inquired at the school but that the tuition (about $1.00 per day) was very expensive. I told her that I was a teacher there and that I would talk to the owner on her behalf. Phung became very excited and thanked me profusely. We chatted for about an hour and then she excused herself because she was late for dinner.

The next day I asked Thérèse about a tuition waiver for Phung. Thérèse became indignant and told me in no uncertain terms that everyone from peasant to president was expected to pay. I offered to pay Phung's tuition but, again, Thérèse would not hear of it. She said that, if other students found out, I would be besieged with requests for me to pay their tuition. I decided that I would give Phung some money quietly so that she could pay the tuition.

Several days later I returned to the business establishment to give Phung the good news. One of the girls told me that Phung was no longer employed there, and didn't know where she could be found. I was very disappointed. I never showed up for dinner at Phung's house and I never saw her again.

Chapter 25
January 1968

Singing in the Rain

In early January 1968, I was made the Assistant Operations Officer at White Birch. I loosely supervised the Morse intercept operators, cryptanalysts, translators, order of battle specialists, and communications traffic analysts.

After I was on the job for about a week, one of the translators came to me and said that he had uncovered a message that looked like "something big was in the works." It was an intercepted radio transmission from COSVN (Central Office, South Vietnam), the North Vietnamese mobile "Pentagon" in South Vietnam to ALL of its subordinate units in South Vietnam. The communiqué told every unit to be ready to receive a very important radio transmission on a particular day at an exact time. **That day was only ten days away!**

Over the past several months, we had intercepted several ominous announcements from upper echelon North Vietnamese units. This fact, coupled with other sources of intelligence, pointed to a high probability that NVA and

Viet Cong units were planning a massive military offensive. Intelligence sources predicted that, if a massive offensive were launched, it would take place during Tet, the Chinese New Year celebrated at the end of January.

Did I have in my hands information pinpointing the date and time that instructions for a Tet offensive would be disseminated to all NVA and Viet Cong units? I shot into action. Immediately I conferred with the Operations Officer and his senior NCO staff. We then electronically notified the appropriate US government agencies of what we had intercepted. We also realized that we had a mere ten days in which to get fully prepared to intercept, decrypt, and translate NVA communications on the appointed day. We formulated a plan in which we would double up on all critical personnel at Operations, cancel all leaves immediately, and put the entire 175th RRC on high alert. Within twenty-four hours we were ready for anything. The entire US intelligence community was also poised to react.

During the remaining nine days, a nervous apprehension pervaded the entire Operations Building. We all felt that we were about to harpoon and capture Moby Dick! I had already identified my best three O58s (Morse Intercept Operators) and they were particularly on edge. Each of them was to work a different portion of the overall NVA communications network.

Fifteen minutes before the appointed time, the operators were geared up and ready. They had tuned into the known frequencies and were just waiting. And then it started! The intercept operators began to produce an avalanche of paper from their mills (typewriters) and it was being immediately turned over to the cryptanalysts. Wait a minute! The transmissions were in plain language, were not encrypted!

What in the hell is going on! I wondered in dismay.

Ten minutes after the initial transmissions began, I was approached by two of the translators.

"Most of the words are not recognizable," they informed me frantically. Neither of them had seen these words nor were any of them in the Vietnamese reference dictionaries that they were using.

I was taken aback. "Let me see what you have," I demanded.

One of the translators handed me a sheet of paper. He had scribbled some of his translation between the lines. However, most of the Vietnamese text was not translated. I looked at the page in a state of panic. I too was at a complete loss. I hurried over to the translation area and grabbed a Vietnamese-English dictionary. I found two words in the dictionary: *âm-giai* (musical scale) and *âm-nhạc* (music). I was deeply puzzled, to say the least. The people around me were beginning to show signs of alarm. And then, I had an idea!

"Let me go take a piss and think about this for a few minutes," I said.

At that moment the Operations Officer came running toward me.

"Well, what does it say?" he barked. "Washington's on my ass for something, right now!" Everyone was now in panic mode, pushing hard to get the answers.

"We're working on it," I responded evasively. We'll have something for them any minute now."

He turned and hurried back to his office. I went into the latrine and looked around. I didn't see anyone else. I stood alone with six sheets of paper in my hand. I stuffed one of the sheets into my uniform shirt and shuffled the others into a pile. I knew full well that these documents were classified Top Secret [Codeword], but I was determined. After waiting another minute or two, I burst out of the latrine, handed the five sheets to the first person I saw, and headed out the front door.

I ran at top speed to the corner, stepped into the street, and hailed a cab. "Tu Do Street and make it fast," I directed the driver in Vietnamese. Within minutes I was standing in front of one of my favorite bars, *The Sportsmen's Club*. Breathlessly I raced in and asked the barmaid for the mamasan, Lien.

At this moment Lien appeared from the kitchen and warmly greeted me.

Frantically I said, "If I ever needed your help, it's now."

"What do you need, Phong?" she asked. Over the past months I knew this woman had developed some affection for me and I was ready to take full advantage of it now.

I motioned to a booth in the back of the bar where the light was dim and we sat down. I unbuttoned several buttons on my shirt and pulled out the wrinkled paper that I had hidden. I pushed it across the table to Lien and she tried to focus on the writing. She motioned to one of the bar girls to bring over a candle from one of the tables up in the front.

"What does it say, sweetheart?" I asked.

She looked and looked at the writing and finally responded, "I see many words I do not understand."

Several of the girls now came forward to look at the paper. They begin to babble to each other trying to somehow figure out what these Vietnamese words meant. After ten minutes of total chaos, I panicked. I grabbed the piece of paper, jumped up from my seat, almost knocked over three of the girls, and bolted for the door. I was dazzled by the bright sunlight and momentarily lost my bearings. And then the gods smiled broadly on me. I had another idea.

I jumped into a cab parked on the curb and yelled "Hai Ba Trung!" The cabbie pulled out into traffic and took off as fast as he could. Fifteen minutes later I arrived at my destination, *The British School*. The gate was locked but I banged on the door and rattled the padlock.

"Who's there?" came a voice from a third floor window of the school.

"It's me, Pierre, and hurry up." My mind raced as fast as my heartbeat. I was so anxious for answers that my words stumbled over themselves.

Two minutes later, Thérèse, school mistress and owner, appeared in a silk bathrobe to unlock the padlock and let me in. I took Thérèse's hand and led her into a classroom nearest the entrance.

I pushed the wrinkled document into her face and exclaimed in no uncertain terms: "I'm screwed if you can't help me out! What is this all about? I don't know most of these words."

She took the document, examined it very closely, and walked to the blackboard. I sat at a desk in the front row. She began to write Vietnamese words on the board with the English translation next to them. The column of English words stunned me: G-clef, musical rest, 4/4 time, quarter note, B-sharp, sixteenth note. She had compiled a list of about fifteen musical terms. I gasped. There it was in front of my nose; the document contained a mixture of words and music. *Holy shit!* I grabbed a crumpled piece of paper out of the wastebasket and wrote down the musical terms faster than any stenographer could have done. I jumped up, gave Thérèse a big hug and kiss, and sped out of the school gate.

She followed after me shouting, "What's this all about? Pierre, Talk to me! Tell me what's happening!"

"I'll let you know when I can" I shouted over my shoulder. The sky had opened up and a heavy squall descended over the city of Saigon. I raced up Hai Ba Trung Street in the general direction of the 175th RRC Operations Building, dodging and weaving around the pedestrians, motorbikes, bicycles, and various obstacles. I was getting soaked so I stopped a "cyclo may" (a wheel chair being pushed by a motorcycle) and jumped in. "Tan Son Nhut!" I bellowed. The driver nodded and took off in a cloud of smoke. During the ride I had to protect the document from getting drenched by the heavy rain by stuffing it in my boot. I unfolded my poncho and kept it draped over my legs.

I had the driver stop about one block from the street leading to the Operations Building at White Birch. I walked the final block, took a deep breath, and entered the building. Ninety minutes had elapsed since I'd left. People were still running around in circles trying to figure out what was contained on the twenty-two pages of intercepted text. When the Operations Officer saw me, he ran over. His face was beet red and he was soaked in sweat although the temperature in the building was about 72°.

"Where in the fuck have you been? You look worse than a wet donkey." Obviously, he could barely contain his annoyance.

"On a little business trip," I responded. I took the crumpled list of musical terms out of my pocket and handed it to the Vietnamese Translation Section Chief, SFC Hilliard. "Here, try this," I suggested.

No one ever asked me again where I had been that afternoon. I think that they understood that some miracle had occurred and they didn't want to jinx it. In the subsequent confusion, I was able to slip the sheet of paper I had in my shirt back into the pile. I would still be on death row at Leavenworth if my superiors had ever found out that I had removed classified material from a secure area without authorization.

Oh Yes! It turned out that the North Vietnamese high command was disseminating to every unit in the field the lyrics and music for the new National Anthem of the Democratic Republic of Vietnam.

Chapter 26
February 1968

An Unexpected Tiger

The Parrot's Beak was a finger of southeast Cambodian territory that jutted into South Vietnam and lies directly at the end of the Ho Chi Minh Trail less than 35 miles from Saigon. The area was sparsely populated, contained mostly dense jungle, but also had several rubber plantations formerly owned by French colonialists. One of its most remarkable features was the sophisticated tunnel and cave complex built during the war with France by the Viet Minh communist guerillas. Impervious to aerial bombardment and artillery, this intricate compound quartered thousands of soldiers and served as an arsenal for military offensives launched by the North Vietnamese. It was from this deadly labyrinth that the Tet Offensive of 1968 was initiated, sending thousands of Viet Cong and North Vietnamese regulars across the border in a failed attempt to capture Saigon, the South Vietnamese capital.

In late February 1968, after the Tet Offensive had run its course, I received orders to go to a small town situated on the Cambodia-South Vietnam border. There I was to interrogate a captured North Vietnamese medical officer and determine the extent of his involve-ment with the enemy troops. U.S. Special Forces operat-ing in the area had stumbled across a large, fully equipped hospital buried in the bowels of a rubber plan-tation. Their official report stated that this subterranean hospital encompassed nearly 6000 square feet, con-tained four operating theaters, forty beds, six of which were used as recovery gurneys, and a sophisticated med-ical laboratory. The entire facility was equipped with the latest French, German, Swiss, and Japanese technology. In short, the hospital was as fine a facility as one might find in any mid-sized American city. Its most unusual feature, however, lay in the fact that the ceiling of the hospital was 8 feet underground and the facility could only be entered via a 100-foot tunnel. The entire hospi-tal was staffed by a commandant, six other doctors, fif-teen nurses, and three lab technicians.

I had been asked to interrogate Colonel Phuong, whose captors had determined that he spoke only French and Vietnamese. Since I was conversant in both lan-guages, I was charged with discovering what the Colonel might know about North Vietnamese troop strengths, lo-cations, armaments, and military objectives. Military In-telligence had trained me well. In language school we had learned the northern Vietnamese dialect, and because we had studied very detailed aerial maps of Hanoi, I knew many of the requisite landmarks and various addresses of buildings. It amazed me that I could talk to someone who had emigrated south from Hanoi in 1954 as if I had myself lived in Hanoi.

We arrived mid-morning in Prasaut, a small town just east of Svay Rieng and about fifty kilometers inside Cambodian territory. I was taken immediately to a white colonial building that served as a jail where Colonel

Phuong was being held. A Special Forces Major escorted me to a "conference" room just inside the door.

"Find out everything you can about this man," I was instructed. "He knows too much about the comings and goings here; too much about Viet Cong and NVA troop locations." It was obvious that my objective was to milk every drop of information from the man who would soon stand before me.

I parked myself in the nearest chair and waited. Several minutes later the Special Forces Major reappeared, this time accompanied by a ramrod-straight officer wearing the NVA uniform of a regular army colonel. The American Major positioned him across from me at the table, saluted, turned and exited the room. The leaden thud of the closing door dropped a curtain on all that remained between me and the familiar world of military protocol.

I sat for a long time while quietly sizing up the colonel as he stared blankly into the empty space that separated us: 35–40 years of age, medium-build, well-composed. The man was obviously not one of the enemy troops slogging through rice paddies! How could I possibly break his resolve? Was this going to be a war of wills? This man was different—had a quality about him that mesmerized me.

Finally, taking a deep breath, I eye-balled him straight on, held out my hand, and said, *"Bonjour, mon Colonel. Je m'appele Capitaine Pierre Fournier. Comment ça va?"*

Because I was an inferior officer, he looked at me directly, an expression of distain spreading across his face. "Don't patronize me, Captain! You don't have to speak French to one who speaks perfectly good English." He leaned back in his chair, obviously comfortable with having the upper hand and proud that he was able to meet me on my own turf.

"Well, well! Let's speak English then," I replied. The colonel's obvious tone of assurance unsettled me.

"Where did you learn English, Sir?"

My jaw dropped as he slowly began to relate his story.

"I am a graduate of Kansas State University and the University of Missouri School of Medicine. I did a residency in orthopedics at Mt. Sinai Hospital in New York City."

"I don't believe you," I rejoined, suddenly aware that his story possibly made sense.

A litany of lies and deceptions encountered in previous interrogations had made me wary of anything not wrapped up in an American flag and tied with yellow ribbons! A knowing grin spread across his face from ear to ear.

Suddenly he stood, waved his arms dramatically as if in the throes of an enthusiastic cheer, and shouted "Mizzou, Mizzou! Go Tigers!"

I was speechless! General disbelief had turned to total amazement.

"Well, I'll be damned," I mumbled. "I think you just might be telling me the truth!"

"Of course, Captain. I always tell the truth."

I gazed squarely into the eyes of this stranger and became a believer!

This astonishing turn of events had me stymied. I took a deep breath and tried to regain my composure. I was desperately eager to connect with this man at a professional officer level, yet here I was, the interrogator, rendered speechless because I had just had the emotional wind knocked out of me. Moments passed.

"Then what in the hell are you doing here?" I asked.

My frustration level rose in proportion to the strange turn of events unraveling before me.

"Obviously, being a doctor to my patients." Colonel Phuong was indignant. "My government asked me to serve, just like yours asked you."

He paused for a moment as if collecting his deepest thoughts.

"It was my patriotic duty to return to the Fatherland and help my people. Nothing personal. Just doing what's right."

Gradually Colonel Phuong's voice began to rise as he spoke of how strongly he felt that the U.S. was an unjust aggressor and that we should "get the hell out" of his country. All he wanted from life was a peaceful existence, a decent home, an education for his children, and an opportunity to serve his people. The more I listened to him, the more I realized that he and I both sought the same things out of life. He was eloquent as he went on to debunk "The Domino Theory" being espoused by our Government in Washington.

"How can we spread Communism to other countries in Southeast Asia," he asked, "when we can't even agree among ourselves exactly what is meant by Communism?"

As he spoke he began to wave his arms for emphasis.

"We are nationalists and all we want is one unified Vietnam under one government."

He paused then, exhausted by the anger that festered within him.

"I never understood why the French wanted to sub-jugate us—and now you Americans think that you have bigger and better answers. Why can't you just leave us alone?"

I was at a loss to respond. Anything I had believed in the past I now called into question in light of our conversation. Right? Wrong? Yes? No? Who had the answers? I tried to get back to the object of this interview, but information about enemy troop strengths and locations no longer seemed as important as the relationship being forged between two men from opposite sides of the world.

His terse response caught me short. "I have no idea about troop strengths and locations. I just treat the wounded. I also try to write letters to the families of soldiers killed in action. That's the least I can do."

"Are you holding out on me, Colonel?" I asked suspiciously in a last feeble attempt to hold onto the upper hand.

He glared at me and declared, "Like I said, Captain. I always tell the truth."

For some unexplained reason, I believed in my heart that this man was incredibly honest and forthright.

"Colonel, I hope that the Americans treat you with the respect that you deserve. You are an honorable man."

I stood up, saluted him (he returned the salute), and left the room. Tears welled up in my eyes as I stumbled blindly toward the jeep. This poignant experience had drained me of any hostile emotion.

Special Forces Major Smith lounged indifferently in the street beside his jeep. The bored expression that underscored the routine nature of his duties turned to eager anticipation as I approached.

"Did you get the goods on him, Captain? When can we get your report?"

Such a naked need to undercut another human being sent shivers up and down my spine and into the arid heat of the day.

Despite the turmoil that raged inside me, I saluted.

"I'll let you know, sir!"

I was in no hurry to file a report or reveal my troubled thoughts to the senior officer who waited so eagerly for news of what had transpired; news that he felt would lead to commendation for himself and his men!

I climbed into the jeep and we sped back toward Saigon in silence. I had been shaken to the core. Mentally I now began to question everything about this war: its strategic purpose, its philosophical purpose, and its political purpose. Personally lukewarm in my support for the war effort, I had, nevertheless, felt compelled to do my duty for my country. I had not yet rationalized whether this was a "just war" or a "political war." It was during this trip back to camp that I became solidly and unambiguously anti-war. Although I felt that I had finally sorted out my loyalties and emotions, the realization of who I had become left me frustrated and despondent. I had lost my taste for the fight.

My report was not what the "Brass" expected, but to the best of my ability I had called the cards as I felt they had been dealt: I had reported that Colonel Phuong was merely doing his duty as prescribed by the Hippocratic Oath. I truly believed Colonel Phuong was politically neutral, a nationalist hero wedged hopelessly in a war of opposing ideologies. Certainly I felt that he didn't have a handle on troop strengths and locations, and that he truly was a man who devoted his life to caring for the sick and wounded. In the end, I put my neck on the line and suggested that he be repatriated to the North.

When my report was read at Battalion headquarters, one would have thought that Captain Peter Fournier had gone to bed with Benedict Arnold, Alger Hiss, and the Rosenbergs. Suddenly I was a prime mover in the Traitor's Hall of Fame! I was told, in no uncertain terms, that the report "needed to be amended" to show what a strategic move the capture of this North Vietnamese officer actually was. I stood by my initial conclusion, however, and held that Colonel Phuong did not have any useful information regarding enemy troop strengths and military logistics. In any case, even if he *had* been privy to this information, it would have been outdated by the time the U.S. army took action—such was the speed and efficiency of the VC and NVA units that were always on the move.

Perhaps my Battalion Commander finally got the message. I found out later on good authority that, although my report was indeed rewritten by one of the Battalion Commander's subordinates, the final version was somehow lost in the bottomless paper trail of military dross.

Chapter 27
May 1968

Penang and Julie, Mes Amours

When I agreed to serve a second year in Vietnam, I had asked my superiors at Battalion headquarters to approve a second R & R for me. They agreed; so, in May of 1968, I took a week's vacation to Penang, Malaysia. I had been told by numerous friends and acquaintances that Penang was truly "heaven on earth." I had also been told by them that I should take advantage of the "marriage broker" system. This was the best way to guarantee great female companionship during the week without the hassle of trolling bars every evening in hopes of finding a girl for the night. Prostitution was illegal in Malaysia and the prostitutes had to be very discreet to avoid the undercover vice police who worked the bars. Also of concern was the high risk of contracting venereal disease.

When our plane landed at the airport, we were greeted by a Navy lieutenant who briefed us on some of the local customs, the currency, the food, and the hotels. We boarded a bus for the fifty-minute ride to the Grand Continental Hotel in Georgetown, the capital. After I checked into the hotel, I took a taxi to Kimberly Street where a dozen shops that supplied female companionship to male tourists were located. I told the taxi driver to stop in the middle of the block and I set out on a walking tour of the area. As I wandered up the narrow street peering in windows and generally enjoying the sounds and sites, a storekeeper rushed to the door of one of the shops and invited me in.

"Sir, are you looking for a wife?" he asked.

His anxious expression left no doubt that he was eager to drum up business.

I nodded yes and he invited me to sit down at a table near the front of the shop. An attractive middle-aged lady appeared and put a pot of tea and two cups on the table. The proprietor, now holding a three-ring binder under his arm, came and stood next to me.

"Sir, welcome to beautiful Penang and all of its delights. I am Mr. Rahman and I have the most beautiful women in all of Asia."

A wide toothy smile spread across his face as he placed the binder on the table and opened it to several photos of young women.

"Pick one of these sexy ladies," he directed. "I will let you look her over."

I looked at the two open pages and pointed to one especially attractive woman. He suggested another equally attractive girl whose photo was at the bottom of the page.

"This woman is special," he informed me. He removed the photo from its plastic slot, and dialed the phone number on the back.

Within five minutes, a gorgeous Eurasian lady walked into the store and I was introduced to Julie. Then

Mr. Rahman instructed her to turn around several times so that I could get a full view of her. He told me that Julie only liked Americans and that she was his most expensive escort.

"How much for this lovely lady?" I asked.

I expected the fee to be way beyond my means.

"Two hundred dollars US for the week," he replied, pleased that I had shown interest and happy that he was about to close a deal.

I didn't know what to say. I had expected $200 for an *hour*. I mumbled my acceptance and began to count out $200 in US currency that I had converted from MPCs at the airport. He stopped me when I had counted out $100.

"No, no! You pay 50% now and 50% later, if you are satisfied."

He reached for the first stack of bills and pushed the rest back toward me. I couldn't believe my ears—a money-back guarantee. In addition, I had fallen instantly in love with this woman who stood quietly on the other side of the table.

Julie and I left the shop hand-in-hand and hailed a cab. As we rode back to my hotel, she told me that she was 21 years old and had been born in Kuala Lumpur of a British mother and a Malay father. She was petite in stature and her bright almond-shaped eyes and waist-length light brown hair accentuated her Western figure. Julie also spoke perfect English with a pronounced British accent. I had hit the jackpot!

Out of the blue she asked me, "Are you married or do you have a special girlfriend?"

This subject was usually never brought up when dealing with Asian women. I was caught off guard and fumbled for a response.

"Yes, I am married but I don't have any children," I said as I averted her eyes.

Julie just nodded and turned her head to look out of the cab window. However, my interest in Julie's personal life was now aroused.

"How about you? Do you have a special man in your life?"

Embarrassed, she responded, "No. Not for two years."

I smiled and changed the subject.

She told me that she needed to stop by her house and "throw a few things" into a suitcase. When we arrived, I waited in the cab until she returned. We then went back to the hotel and I carried Julie's luggage up to the room. From my hotel window we watched the ferries transporting passengers back and forth to the mainland from the island of Penang. In the distance I could see miles of majestic beaches and the emerald waters of the bay. On the horizon were ships of all sizes and descriptions: Chinese junks, tankers, sailboats, yachts, and houseboats all vying for their own maritime space in the Strait of Molucca.

Suddenly, I was brought back to my surroundings by the voice of an angel. I turned around and looked across the room.

"Peter, come here. I need to speak with you."

Julie sat on the edge of the bed and was patting the sheets to invite me to sit next to her. She began to unbutton my shirt and kiss me all over my face. We fell into each other's arms.

Two hours later, after we had showered and dressed, Julie suggested that we go out and get something to eat. She knew all of the small ethnic restaurants where we could eat authentic Chinese, Filipino, Indian, and Malaysian cuisine far from where the milling tourists congregated. Following her lead, we ate well for a fraction of what the tourists would have spent.

During the week, she also took me to shops where she bargained on my behalf for jewelry, clothing, Indonesian batik cloth, and Thai silk. As was expected, I repaid her with clothing and jewelry along the way.

In return, I enjoyed a doting companion whose desire was to satisfy my every whim. I walked and played in Shangri-La with an elegant, classy, and sexy woman. Julie was extremely passionate and put her heart and soul into *everything* that we did. On most days we were so tired out we did not get up until noon.

On our last night together, we chose to dine in a small intimate restaurant tucked away on a side street. Both of us were saddened by the knowledge that I would leave the following day. We had just clinked glasses to propose a toast when a man heading for an empty table accidentally bumped into Julie's chair. The impact knocked the glass out of her hand; it bounced off the edge of the table and smashed onto the floor. In the process, several ice cubes fell into the front of Julie's low-cut blouse. She jumped up as if shocked by a jolt of electricity. The table overturned sending all of the chinaware and food skidding across the tile floor. Julie began to hop up and down as if possessed by the devil.

A waiter came running to assist us, but when he saw what was happening, he backed off. He did not want to be seen with his hand in the wrong place on a woman. I tried to help but, again, I did not want to do something indelicate in a public place. I yelled for Julie to run to the ladies' room. The waiter kept pointing in that direction. She hurried toward the ladies room, "oohing" and "aahing" all the way.

As soon as she was out of sight, I broke out laughing. Five waiters were trying to right the table, pick up the pieces of chinaware and food, and restore order. They were all apologizing at once to me. I kept telling them that it was an accident and that they should not worry. I also noticed that the man who caused the entire problem had disappeared.

The other patrons in the restaurant were talking animatedly and pointing. This was apparently the most excitement some of them had had in a long time. Mr. George, the owner of the restaurant, came over and apologized repeatedly. He kept asking me if I was "alright."

"Yes," I assured him. "No one has been injured."

I was beginning to feel uncomfortable at his repeated inquiries.

"When your lady returns, I will seat you in my private dining room," he insisted.

"That's not necessary. The only harm has been to a young lady's dignity," I responded.

When Julie returned the entire front of her dress was wet and she looked as if she had seen a ghost. The owner kept apologizing. She assured him that everything was OK, and that we would have to leave so that she could change her clothes. Mr. George insisted that he would take care of everything if we accepted his offer of dining in his private dining room.

Julie protested. "I can't eat in this wet dress!" she exclaimed.

She was clearly distraught and anxious to leave.

The owner replied, "You must trust me. Everything will be OK."

He showed us to the private dining room. Five minutes later a young woman came in carrying several garments.

"Mr. George says for you to choose one of these outfits," the woman stated.

She unfolded three beautiful Indonesian batik skirts with matching tops for Julie to examine.

"How much?" Julie inquired.

She was embarrassed by all of the attention being lavished on her.

"Compliments of Mr. George," the lady responded.

Julie pointed to one of the outfits. I told her to go back to the ladies room and put on the new outfit. Minutes later she emerged, even more stunning than before. Three waiters had been assigned to wait on us. Mr. George himself acted as the headwaiter. He brought a bottle of champagne and we ate and drank to our heart's content. When we had finished, I asked for the check.

"No check," he responded.

I insisted on paying, at least for the champagne. Julie whispered to me that Mr. George would be insulted if I refused his offer. I reluctantly gave in.

On our way back to the hotel, we walked barefoot on the beach and kissed many times. No fairy princess could have looked lovelier in the moonlight than the elegant Julie; no movie script could have provided a more fantastic conclusion to the magic of the evening. Julie even proposed marriage to me. I sadly repeated what I had already told her. She broke down and cried uncontrollably.

Frustrated, she threw her shoes into the surf and ran back to the hotel. When I arrived back at the room, Julie was already in bed under the sheets. I undressed and slipped in beside her. Our naked bodies touched.

When I awoke the next morning, Julie was gone. She had left a note on hotel stationery with her name and address and a tender goodbye message.

Peter,
    I love you so much—I will cry every night.
Come back soon to me.

Love forever,

Julie

I was totally depressed. I packed, dressed, took a cab to the "marriage" shop, and paid the remaining $100. The proprietor thanked me profusely and complimented me on how kind and considerate I had been to Julie, his eldest daughter.

Chapter 28
July 1968

Playing With Fire

The Operations Center at Tan Son Nhut was a spacious facility that boasted of the finest state-of-the-art communications and computer equipment. Formerly known as the 175th Radio Research Company, the unit had been re-designated as the US Army Security Agency Operations Company, Saigon in December 1967; later, in July 1968, the Company was relocated to Bien Hoa and re-designated as the USASA Operations Company, Bien Hoa. Administratively, we now came under the 303rd Radio Research Battalion in Long Binh (Camp LBJ).

In January 1968, I had been promoted to Captain O-3, and assigned as the Assistant Operations Officer at the Bien Hoa facility. Five months later my superior officer informed me that a high-powered inspection party was coming from Arlington Hall Station, Virginia, to look over our new facilities. He also advised me that prior to their arrival we would receive a list of officers who held Top Secret clearances and who were thus "cleared for access" to our building. By mail we would receive photographs of each of these official inspectors and our

Security Officer would then create photo IDs for these men to wear while they were inside our secure facilities. Since the visit wasn't scheduled until the third week of July, it seemed feasible that this paperwork could be processed in plenty of time.

Photos and documents delivered over the next three weeks indicated that the inspection team was comprised of one captain, one major, two lieutenant colonels, and one full colonel and that these officers would visit from July 26 through July 31. Excited to have an opportunity to prove our professionalism to headquarters, the entire unit set about ways to demonstrate our organizational skills and our commitment to the mission.

On the morning of July 26 the inspection entourage arrived. As Assistant Operations Officer, I was on hand to greet them with the Company Commander, the Company Executive Officer, the Operations Officer, the Senior NCO, and various other Operations personnel. As we stood in formation, I saluted each in turn—and then it hit me. There were SIX officers. I counted again. Yep, there were six officers! Instead of *one,* there were *two* full colonels in the group.

Flustered I distributed the photo ID badges and came up one short. How could this have happened? I asked to see the original access paperwork. Someone ran back into Operations and returned with the folder. I read and reread its contents several times. No matter how I looked at it, Colonel Goodman was not on the list. The significance of this "oversight" was enormous for, according to Army Regulation, IF YOU'RE NOT ON THE ACCESS LIST, YOU DON'T HAVE ACCESS!! Colonel Goodman would not be allowed to enter the Operations building!

When I informed the Company Commander of the situation, we decided that there must have been a mistake. "My God, Sir, what are we going to do with this one?"

I could envision rounds of questionings and reprimands being handed out to every man in the unit.

"Arlington Hall is going to be very pissed when they find out about our apparent screw-up," he snorted. "On the other hand, Fournier, I think that our paperwork covers our asses."

I agreed whole-heartedly. "From what I can see, Sir, we're fully covered!"

I breathed a sigh of relief, thoroughly convinced that we had religiously carried it off according to Hoyle.

"We did everything by the goddam book! If my hunch is correct, Arlington Hall has just put one Colonel Goodman in a downright embarrassing situation. And, guess who's in the middle?"

I laughed at his reply, "Fournier, I think that if we didn't have bad luck, we wouldn't have any luck at all!"

Ever the realist, my CO could always bring you down to earth!

"Well, what now, Sir? Shall we fall on our swords now or later?"

I knew we had to act quickly, and I was glad the decision would rest with someone else.

"Shit! We need to stall for time, Fournier. Ask the party to take a break and report back at 1300."

I agreed that we needed a window of time to send a message to Arlington Hall and determine if a mistake had been made.

As fast as our jungle boots could carry us, the CO and I high-tailed it to the communications shed and pounded out a message to Camp Zama, Japan.

"HAVE VISITOR, COL. G. GOODMAN. NOT ON YR ACCESS LST. PLS ADVISE."

Ninety agonizing minutes later a chilling reply stared up at us: "DENY ACCESS. GOODMAN CLRNCE UNDER REV[IEW]."

Several hours later, the six members of the inspection team returned to the Operations area. Since I was the Assistant Operations Officer, I was elected to inform Colonel Goodman that he would have to wait outside while the other five members of the team entered the building.

I approached the Colonel, saluted, and announced, "Sorry, Sir. But Arlington Hall Station has denied your clearance."

The Colonel's face flamed an angry crimson as he hoisted himself to his full height of six-foot-two, planted himself directly in my path, and fumed in a voice that sent daggers through me.

"I don't give a damn what they say at the Hall, Captain! I didn't come 12,000 miles to stand here in the broiling sun and wait for a bunch of half-assed nitwits to unscrew the mess they've made of my records. I'm headed in!"

Struggling to maintain control of the situation, I suggested that he talk directly with Arlington Hall Station and offered to assist him. But to no avail.

He shoved me aside and raged, "I don't need to talk to those sons-of-bitches. I have a clearance and I'm coming in."

Angrily he paced back and forth in front of me, a man obviously agitated and determined to use physical force, if necessary.

"Get out of my way!" he screamed.

I braced myself for the onslaught.

"Sir," I replied. "I'm very sorry but you are not authorized to enter this building and it's my duty to enforce the regulations."

Suddenly I became aware that my CO, XO, and the other five officers had crowded around us.

"Chicken shit!"

One of the Lt. Colonels stepped forward to take Colonel Goodman's side. He berated me in scathing tones.

"Who the hell do you think you are, refusing to obey a superior officer? You're nothing but a low-grade shit of a junior officer!"

My CO stepped up to diffuse the furor quickly escalating before our eyes.

Respectfully he stated, "We have a job to do here, Sir. I support Captain Fournier. Goodman will not be allowed to enter our Operations Building."

As if on cue, the second Colonel stepped into the discussion.

He looked directly at me and charged, "I order you to allow Colonel Goodman to accompany our party during this visit to the Operations Building."

He was tall, menacing, and definitely used to having his way.

Though the last thing I wanted was a face-off with top brass, I squared my shoulders, took a deep breath, and spat out my reply. "NFW[1], Sir!"

Visions of an impending court-martial flashed before my eyes, but I stood my ground and stepped forward to block the Colonel's path.

Emboldened by the show of support from his companions, Goodman now threatened in earnest.

"Outta my way, gentlemen. I'm going in. Try to stop me, and you'll have me and Betsy here to deal with."

He pointed to the .45 caliber pistol at his side.

Naked fear shot through me then, but I looked directly into the Colonel's eyes.

"I will now instruct the guard to take all necessary and sufficient action to prevent you from entering the building," I threatened.

Holding my breath, I turned slowly and walked into the foyer of the building. Once inside, I instructed the military policeman on duty that, under no circumstances, should a Colonel Goodman be allowed into the building.

"Be prepared to take whatever action is appropriate to prevent unauthorized entry," I directed.

I took the guard out front and pointed Goodman out to him. He in turn radioed the MP Sergeant-of-the-Guard and the Officer- of-the-Day (OID) to come at once.

Outside the argument had erupted into a violent shouting match compounded by idle threats, wild gesturing,

---

1. Army lingo for "No Fucking Way".

and a rash of random finger pointing. Within fifteen minutes, however, the MPs, the OID, and several other officers descended on the scene as a unified force. I briefed them quickly and stepped aside. The OID went over to Colonel Goodman, saluted, and asked if he could do anything to help alleviate the situation. Goodman, however, was out of control. His contorted face had turned beet red leaving no doubt that he was determined to pull rank and get his way.

"I'm going in and no one's going to stop me," Goodman stormed.

We had reached a point of no return. I stepped foreword, shook my head emphatically and warned him one last time.

"Sir, you are not authorized to enter this building; the guard has been ordered to use whatever force necessary to prevent your entry."

Never in my life had I dared to address a senior officer in this way, yet here I was thrown into the nasty jaws of an impending disaster.

Colonel Goodman spat on the ground, brushed past the other inspectors, and headed straight for the entrance of the Operations Building. As one, we moved to block his approach as he steamed up the concrete sidewalk and headed toward the bewildered guard, who now visibly unsnapped the top of his holster.

"Out of my way, soldier," Goodman demanded.

"Sir, you are not authorized to enter and I will use all means at my disposal to prevent your entry."

The young recruit dutifully repeated my command. His repeated warnings had obviously had not hit their mark. The colonel merely glared around the circle and impaled each one of us with a look of daggers.

"Get out of my way," Goodman barked and took two steps toward the entrance.

The guard removed his pistol from its holster and pointed it at the ground. The die had been cast and I felt completely powerless to defuse this situation. I glanced at the guard, I glanced at Goodman, I glanced at the ground. My head spun with alternatives. *Should I let the situation dictate the outcome? Should I jump Goodwin and pin him to the ground so that we could handcuff him? Should we try to contact someone on General Westmoreland's staff?* I could see no clear way out!

"Are you threatening me?" snorted Goodman.

The Colonel was out of control and completely beyond reason. He had lost the last thread of authority that had held me in its bond of respect.

"Colonel, any other words just won't do. You are not authorized to enter and I will use all means at my disposal to prevent your entry."

All of a sudden a wave of calm washed over me. No matter what I did, I had fellow officers and the Army regulations behind me. I became resolute and authoritative. I was going to seize the situation and take whatever actions were necessary. I had had enough bullshit from every quarter. Now I decided to follow my intuition right or wrong!

"Take one more step, Sir, and he'll have to shoot you!"

The Colonel lunged forward in a desperate attempt to wrench the gun away from the guard. A loud crack split the air sending a bullet into Colonel Goodman's right bicep. Clutching his arm, the startled Goodman fell to the ground writhing in pain. The look in his eye was one of utter disbelief. He kept checking his bloodied arm, the guard, me, and the people assembled nearby. Clearly he was unable to focus on anything or anybody.

From this point on all hell broke loose.

"Get an ambulance!" one officer screamed.

The Colonel, thrashing about on the ground, bellowed that he had been shot and vowed swift and unremitting vengeance. A nearby soldier ripped open the Colonel's shirt and tore long strips that he promptly applied as a tourniquet. Within minutes an ambulance screeched to a halt beside the now semi-conscious Colonel Goodman. The medics hoisted him to his feet, piled him into the vehicle and sped away. I looked for the guard.

The young man stood alone against a wall and quietly sobbed. I went over and put my arm around his shoulder.

"You did the right thing, soldier," I consoled.

Underneath the tears, however, I could see a faint smile.

He leaned very close and whispered, "You know, sir, I always knew that I might have to do this someday. It was easier than I thought."

The following month a Board of Inquiry was convened. People came from Camp Zama and from the U.S. to look into this incident. Everyone even vaguely associated with the confrontation was interviewed and re-interviewed. As for me, the mountains of paperwork I had to face overwhelmed me. Twenty hours of testimony left me drained and depressed. It seemed as if Whitman and I had written enough material to fill volumes A–J of the Encyclopedia Britannica. In the end, however, we were all exonerated. Colonel Goodman was severely reprimanded and forced to retire in disgrace from the Army. One week after the incident, my time in Vietnam expired. I returned to the States desperate to recover some semblance of normalcy.

Five years later I learned what had been going on with Colonel Goodman. He had had a chronic spinal disc problem and had been taking increasingly potent painkillers to ease the pain. Finally he had wheedled and cajoled an Army doctor into prescribing codeine and Demerol. On his own, Colonel Goodman had taken to smoking marijuana when the pain became intolerable. The good Colonel had become one gigantic drug addict and fearing reprisals, his doctor "friend" had alerted the authorities.

No doubt Colonel Goodman was flying high on that fateful day in Vietnam. That also explains why Arlington Hall Station was re-evaluating his security clearance. Though hindsight leads us to view the incident a little more kindly, in my heart of hearts, I will always believe that we did the right thing on that fateful day in Bien Hoa.

Chapter 29
March 1970

Trouble in Terpdom

Shortly after my military discharge, in September 1968, I entered the University of Maryland in College Park. I had previously accumulated about two year's worth of credits and I figured that I could get my bachelor's degree in less than two years by attending year 'round. I hoped to pursue my dream of becoming a doctor so I took a heavy load of chemistry, zoology, physics, and mathematics. Life was good. I was attending college on the GI Bill and my wife had a prestigious job at the National Security Agency as a Chinese linguist/analyst. We lived in an upscale three-bedroom, two-bath townhouse in Columbia, Maryland.

By March 1970 I was looking forward to graduation in May. Suddenly the University dropped a bombshell: I was in danger of not graduating because I owed a large sum of money and I lacked credits in two mandatory areas. Since the University rules stated that one's state of residency is the state from which one entered military service, and I had enlisted in New Jersey, I was classified as a non-resident for tuition purposes. Therefore, said the "powers that be," I should have been paying out-of-state tuition. Subsequently, I owed them about $6,000 dollars. The required credits I lacked were in the areas of language and physical training. I didn't know whether to laugh or cry.

I wrote to the administration and pointed out that I owned property in Maryland, I paid Maryland state income tax, my cars were registered in Maryland, and I lived permanently at a Maryland address. In a separate letter I dealt with the two other issues. I described in detail my language training and military duties. I also pointed out that soldiers do an enormous amount of physical training.

Within one week I had my responses. Their decision that I was a resident of New Jersey would stand. Also, since Vietnamese was not taught by any of the language departments at the University, my "outside" language training would not count. They even had the audacity to make a reference to "Berlitz." However, they would graciously waive the physical training requirement due to my military service.

I was so angry I couldn't see straight. I talked the situation over with my wife and my parents and we decided to sue the University. I also contacted the language-training department at the National Security Agency to see if they could help. I got in touch with a local lawyer who told me that he was not interested in taking the case. When I asked him if he knew another lawyer who might be interested, he said that he didn't. *Why did I feel I was about to be screwed?* I figured that I had to do something myself. So, I boldly asked the University if I could plead my case at the next meeting of the Board of Regents. To my surprise they agreed to my request. The following week I received an official document from the National Cryptologic School at Ft. Meade. It showed that they were accredited by the Commission on Accreditation of Service Experiences of the American Council on Education to teach languages. My year of Vietnamese language training was equivalent to 36 college credits (1820 contact hours, 7 hours per day, 5 days per week for 52 weeks). I was ecstatic! Now, the only hurdle I had to get over was the residency issue.

On the appointed evening, my wife and I drove to Baltimore for the 7:30 P.M. meeting at the University of Maryland School of Law. When we arrived, we were told that the Board had business to discuss and that we would have to wait about an hour.

At 8:30 P.M., I was called into the Boardroom and was introduced to the nine members of the Board of Regents. Immediately I recognized one of the members, Trent Schultz, the Board student representative who, coincidentally, had been my Organic Chemistry lab partner. *I thought that some unbelievable chain of events was about to unfold!* He made believe that he had never seen me before, and made sure that we did not make eye contact.

The Chairman of the Board read a statement explaining why I was there and said, "Mr. Fournier, please proceed and state your case."

I basically read the letter that I had sent previously and I gave each member a copy of the document from the National Cryptologic School. I talked for about ten minutes.

When I had finished, the Chairman asked the members, "Do any of you have any questions for Mr. Fournier?"

Everyone shook their heads negatively. I felt that I had not done a good job.

The Chairman told me, "Please wait outside while this Board votes."

After a mere three minutes, I was invited back into the Boardroom. I was sweating like a pig! The vote had been tallied and I held my breath.

The Chairman's brief speech went something like: "Mr. Fournier. The Board of Regents of the University of Maryland has considered your request for residency status and for credit for Vietnamese language study. We have voted to grant you residency status and to direct that your academic transcript reflect 36 academic credits. Congratulations!"

I almost jumped up and kissed each of them. When the meeting adjourned shortly thereafter, Trent Schultz came over to shake my hand.

He told me in a loud whisper, "Pete, I recognized you immediately but I did not want the other Board members to know that I knew you. They would have asked me to excuse myself from any voting. As it was, the final vote was 5–4!"

"Hey, man, you saved my life in there," I exclaimed.

"Pete, you saved my butt several times in Organic Chem," he replied. "Also, the Board is also going to recommend to the State Legislature that the law be changed to reflect exceptions to the residency rules and to what constitutes academic credit for military language training."

I later found out that the Maryland State Legislature passed what was dubbed the "Fournier Rule" to give relief to others whose circumstances might parallel mine.

I considered this a fitting end to my long and arduous stint in the military. From peacocks to brothels, from teahouses to trenches, I'd seen it all. The good morphed with the bad, but always I live with a memory of these years that shaped my life. IT HAD BEEN ONE HELLUVA RIDE!!!

Appendix

Peter Fournier Timeline

February 1964	Joined the Army
February 1964– April 1964	Basic Training, Ft. Dix, NJ
May 1964– November 1964	Comm. Traffic Analysis School, Ft. Devens, MA
November 1964– March 1965	Republic of the Philippines
April 1965– April 1966	Language School
June 30, 1966	Commissioned as 2nd Lieutenant, O-1, assigned as Unit Laundry & Morale Officer
January 3, 1967	Promoted to 1st Lieutenant, O-2, and assigned as Exec. Officer of 175th RRU
May 1966– April 1967	Republic of Vietnam
May 1967	Extended one year in Vietnam One-month leave
June 1967– June 1968	Republic of Vietnam

January 6, 1968	Promoted to Captain, O-3, and assigned as Asst. Operations Officer at 175th RRU
July 1968	Returned to States, discharged as Captain, O-3
September 1968	Entered University of Maryland